Gibson®

MASTERTONE

FLATHEAD 5-STRING BANJOS OF THE 1930'S AND 1940'S

BY JIM MILLS

BOOK LAYOUT AND COVER DESIGN BY JIM FILIPPI

ISBN 978-1-57424-246-1
SAN 683-8022

P.O. Box 17878 Anaheim Hills, CA 92817
www.centerstream-usa.com

COURTESY THE JIM MILLS COLLECTION

RARE COLOR PHOTO OF LULU BELLE & SCOTTY WISEMAN, CIRCA 1950'S. SCOTTY IS HOLDING AN RB-18 WITH CATLIN BUTTON TUNERS LIKE THE RB-18 FEATURED IN CHAPTER 19 OF THIS BOOK.

Table of Contents

Foreword 4

Introduction 6

Acknowledgements 9

Chapter One The Willie Bivens RB-3 Wreath 10

Chapter Two The Orval Britton RB-3 16

Chapter Three "The African Queen" The Rob Tarnow "No Hole" RB-3 20

Chapter Four The Butch Robbins RB-4 28

Chapter Five The Snuffy Jenkins RB-4 34

Chapter Six The Sonny Osborne RB-Granada 42

Chapter Seven The Earl Scruggs RB-Granada 48

Chapter Eight The Hoke Jenkins RB-6 60

Chapter Nine The Bill Worrell RB-75 68

Chapter Ten The Mack Crow Gold Plated RB-75 76

Chapter Eleven "Nellie" The Don Reno RB-75 86

Chapter Twelve The J. D. Crowe RB-75 96

Chapter Thirteen The Posie Roach RB-75 104

Chapter Fourteen The Curtis McPeake RB-75 "Ole Betsy" 110

Chapter Fifteen The Steve Huber RB-75 116

Chapter Sixteen The Last RB-75? 122

Chapter Seventeen The Hubert Loar RB-7 126

Chapter Eighteen The RB-12 130

Chapter Nineteen The RB-18 134

An Economic History of the Gibson Pre War Flathead Fivestring Mastertone banjo. 138

Major Cosmetic Differences between early to mid 1930's Mastertones, when compared to late 1930's and early 1940's style 75's and Toptension Banjos 158

Other Stuff Besides Banjos 160

The First Appearance of the Flathead Tonering in Print and Standard Factory Production 164

Some Known Serial Numbers of Original Gibson Flathead Fivestring Mastertone Banjos 169

Foreword

The first Original Flathead Fivestring Mastertone that I ever laid my hands on completely ruined me from that day forward. I was only 14 years old, setting in the floor "Indian style" in Harry West's living room.

Harry West and his beautiful wife Jeanie had recently moved to my hometown, the Raleigh / Durham area of North Carolina, and were only a 20 minute drive from my house. Since I still wasn't old enough to drive, my dad took me over there. After introductions, Harry started bringing out the usual stuff that he figured my dad could afford, like the better quality newer banjos, and a few Pre War Gibson conversion banjos, etc., and I guess after hearing me get around pretty good on those banjos, he decided to bring out the Real Deal ...an Original 1930's Fivestring Flathead Mastertone, RB-3 Wreath pattern!

I can tell you that, as a dealer he made a terrible mistake right there.... because 15 seconds after wrapping my hands around that Original Flathead RB-3, I had absolutely no interest in anything else he had to offer! All I remember is "the sound" coming out of that banjo. It seemed like the sound was almost coming deep out of the ground somewhere when compared to all the other banjos I'd played before.

Needless to say we didn't buy anything that day, but over the course of the next few years I got to know Harry and Jeanie well, and when I would come and visit with them, Harry would simply turn me loose in what I called my "dream room" where all the good stuff was. I'm talking about stuff like Pre War Martin D-45's, and many 1930's Herringbone D-28's, several Gibson F-5 Loar period mandolins, and of course the main thing that I was interested in, that Original Flathead Fivestring RB-3. Of course at that age I was trying to learn to play everything, and Harry would just let me play anything my heart desired, for as long as I wanted to. I would grab a Loar mandolin for a while, put it down and pick up a Pre War Martin guitar, but I'd always end up with that Flathead banjo the longest.

I was very fortunate to also get to play several local shows with Harry and Jeanie throughout the summer when I was out of school, and it was always a lot of fun to be on stage with them.

One day I asked Harry what made him decide to start collecting vintage stringed instruments way back in the 1940's and 50's, and he told me a little story that I thought was really interesting that I've never forgotten. I truly believe it sums up why any of us collect these particular banjos and other vintage stringed instruments. Harry said he'd been playing music for a while by the early 1940's and had owned several used 1930's Martin D-28 Herringbones. He'd simply pick them up when he could find them for $75.00 to $100.00 in pawn shops or wherever. He'd play them for a while and then sell them for a few dollars profit later on. In 1944 he decided to buy himself a brand new Martin D-28 guitar, and ordered one. When it arrived he noticed right away that this new guitar was nowhere near as good as the older 1930's model D-28's that he'd owned. It just didn't have that same "sound". So from then on, he began hanging onto these old guitars whenever he found them, and selling off other things that he didn't like as well. This led to his taking notice of more "sounds", and purchasing even more instruments like 1930's and 40's Gibson Mastertone banjos, and of course 1920's F style Gibson mandolins, and that's basically the story of how America's "first" dealer in Vintage Stringed Instruments got started.

HARRY & JEANIE WEST CIRCA 1960'S

I just think that's such a great story because, as you can see, it's always been about "the sound" from the very beginning...

That "sound" is as honest as it gets folks.
It always tells the truth and cannot lie.
Money cannot affect it.

I don't care how rare an instrument is, or how much it's supposed to be worth monetarily, if it doesn't have that "sound" then it's not going to ring true with you or anyone else either.

And that is exactly why these particular banjos have stood the test of time for over 75 years now..."They have the Sound" And I've found no other way in this world to obtain it. **PERIOD.**

I would like to thank Mr. Harry West for my early informal education long ago on these wonderful instruments, allowing me hands on knowledge of them at such a young age. I can look back today **NEARLY 30 YEARS** later, and realize that every 14 year old kid doesn't get an opportunity like that, and I'm very appreciative and thankful to him for it.

That first experience helped lead me through life to the book you now have in your hands today.

ENJOY

Sincerely,

Jim Mills

Introduction

A book of this sort was something that I'd hoped would have been available many years ago, written by someone qualified and willing to write it. After all, there were already several books authored on Pre War Martin and Gibson guitars of every kind, and also an extensive journal in book form of every known Gibson F-5 Lloyd Loar signed Mandolin, and several other books on many great American stringed instruments, but basically nothing existed in print, that focused entirely on these extremely rare and collectable banjos. The thing that got me was, there seemed like some secret society of collectors, and players, that were completely consumed by these banjos, but unwilling to write or share any information concerning these wonderful pieces of Americana. It seems another problem was finding someone interested enough to take the time and effort required in finding photographers, and setting up photo shoots all over the country, then researching, traveling to see them, and writing such an in depth document. Then to have the even larger dilemma of finding a publisher willing to take a chance on a book like this, in such uncharted waters.

There's a sizable amount of folks all over this Country and throughout the world, collecting, trading, and compiling information on these rare banjos, including several that I refer to as "Scholars". You'll notice that I don't recognize anyone as an "Expert" on these banjos, that's because I don't know of anyone who's seen everything. I believe there is a never ending opportunity to learn something new concerning these extremely rare and interesting instruments. It seems I see something completely original, yet totally unprecedented with each New Year. Therefore I consider all of us seeking this information, as merely scholars in this endeavor. I'll also have to report that our overall knowledge has increased greatly as a whole, in just the past 15 years. This is especially true in the small details, such as dating banjos from original factory shipping records, original Bills of Sale, model designation, and inlay patterns, etc. For example twenty years ago the term RB-75 was virtually unheard of by all but a few of the most serious students of the Pre War Gibson banjo. If it was a mahogany, nickel plated Mastertone banjo from the 1930's, it was considered a style 3, and that was that. If it had a flying eagle inlay pattern it was a style 4, if it was gold plated it was a Granada, and that was that. For many years, several famously owned, and well known banjos were falsely identified in print, simply because of a general lack of knowledge concerning these details. Now for instance, since so much new information has come to light, we are aware that there were many different variations of the style 75 banjos, with different wood types, and various inlay patterns, and even mixed plating's on the same banjo. A lot of good has also come from the advent of the internet and has made it possible for more folks all over the world to communicate on these subjects more easily. The website www.earnest-banjo.com, is owned and operated by my good friend Greg Earnest, and deserves a world of credit for furthering the interest and also further educating folks about these fine instruments.

I sincerely hope that this book even though not a full history on all of Gibson's wonderful Pre War banjos, would spark a new fire in many, creating enough interest, that they would decide to educate us further, by researching and writing many more books and documentaries concerning these extremely rare banjos, therefore increasing our knowledge, and also keeping them and their unmatched sound alive and well for future generations.

Concerning the writing of this book, it just so happens, I had written a few articles on these wonderfully rare banjos, that were published in Bluegrass Unlimited Magazine over a two or three year period. One of these articles was read by a fellow named Ron Middlebrook, who I'll have to say, went the extra mile to track me down. Ron is a very passionate man when it comes to America, and also vintage American stringed instruments. Mr. Middlebrook is the owner and President of Centerstream Publishing LLC, which has published many instructional books, DVDs, and complete History books on several American stringed instrument companies. He proceeded to tell me that he just had to find me, and tell me how much he enjoyed reading my article. He made me an open offer, right then and there, to write the book you now have in your hands. I'll have to say that no one could have been more surprised than I, when he called, and I want to thank him here publically for his interaction that's made all of this possible.

The first person I thought of when I agreed to write the book was fellow banjo Scholar and professional photographer Dan Loftin. I had admired Dans great photography for several years in the fine book, "Acoustic Guitars and other Fretted Instruments", by George Gruhn and Walter Carter, and also several other publications. His attention to detail and clarity is impeccable. He also happens to be a fine banjo picker, and has owned several original flatheads. I know my first question to him concerning whether he'd take this job must have sounded a little odd..."How much would it cost me to get you to go on a 4 day road trip, through three states, to shoot around 15 banjos in different people's homes?" He thought for a few minutes and had an answer for me, to which I replied, you're hired!

Dan and I had a ball traveling in a rental car for the better part of 4 days, eating at Waffle Houses, sleeping in cheap hotels, telling each other our life's histories, but mainly talking about Pre War Gibson banjos almost nonstop. I couldn't have picked a better companion for such a trip. He also had great ideas concerning angles, and lighting for cumbersome banjo photos. I don't know if many of you have ever tried to take a simple photo of a banjo, but it doesn't exist. First of all, there's nothing photo friendly about a banjo! Everything is against you from the start. The plating whether nickel, chrome, or gold, can create a hot spot in the flash in nearly every position, and you usually don't know it's there until you print the photo. The resonators are all curved in a way which refracts light. This can turn out images crazier than any fun house mirror you've ever seen! It's not an easy task to get really good quality photos of Pre War Gibson Banjos.

Also, most of these banjos were owned by individuals, some still in the original owners families. These folks were not too keen on riding their precious banjos across the country for photographing, so we had to go to them. I'll have to say that I worked Dan pretty hard, going into complete stranger's homes, convincing them that we would arrange their living room furniture back where we found it, after we were through photographing their banjos! Dan had to deal with, dogs, cats, children, and homes with little or no natural light. We traveled down countless miles of winding 2 lane country roads, and several dirt roads, in a car loaded full of his fragile and expensive photography equipment. Not to mention fighting record setting temperatures of over 100 degree heat, the whole week we set out to get all this done. Through it all, he handled every situation perfectly, and for that I'm mighty grateful to him. I sincerely hope you the reader, enjoy this book as much as I've enjoyed writing it. It was a labor of love, and I do mean labor, but well worth the time and effort that went into it.

Being able to bring a book like this to the whole Pre War Gibson banjo community of collectors, players, and enthusiast like myself, who've wanted such a documentary for many years, has been one of the true highlights of my life.

Sincerely,

JimMills

COURTESY THE JIM MILLS COLLECTION

MY GRANDADDY..."RUSSELL HUGH MILLS" CIRCA 1960'S, ABOUT THE TIME I WAS BORN! MAYBE I COULD HEAR HIS BANJO BEFORE THEN...

Acknowledgements

None of this book would have been possible without the help and support of my many friends and colleagues throughout the Pre War Gibson banjo world. Some are simply players, some are dealers and collectors, but I'll just call them all my friends. I would like to thank them here publically for all their knowledge, friendship, and willingness to help throughout the years:

Earl Scruggs, J D Crowe, Sonny Osborne, Ralph Stanley, Curtis McPeake, George Gruhn, Harry West, Pete Kuykendall, Darrell McCumbers, Steve Huber, Walter Carter, Dan Loftin, Sam Calveard, Frank Neat, Snuffy Smith, David Wadsworth, Stan Werbin, John Bernunzio, Greg Earnest, Tom Biggs, Harold Chriscoe, John Hedgecoth, Larry Perkins, Jerry Keys, Dave Osborne, Nowell Creadick, Frank Godbey, Dick Powell, Frank Schoepf, Jim Burlile, Jimmy Cox, Clarence Green, Ranger Doug Green, Gibson Inc., Wayne Holcomb, Doug Hutchens, Mike Longworth, Ken Landreth, Mandolin Bothers Inc., Walt Pittman, Frank Ray, Greg Rich, Mike Seeger, R. C. Snoddy, Dave Sweet, Tony Williamson, DAWG, Jim Yarboro, Rual Yarborough, Andy Cartoun, Leonard Coulson, Tom McKinney, Tut Taylor, Al Amisano, Joe Davisson, Bob Anderson, Paul Hopkins, Charlie Cushman, Clarence Hall, Ray Whisnant, Wayne Bridges, Eric Ellis, Jim Rollins, Melvin Cumbee, all the families and folks who allowed us to photograph their banjos for this book, and many others I'm sure I've forgotten. Please forgive me.

Thank you all, and God Bless you.

Sincerely,

Jim Mills

The Willie Bivens
RB-3 Wreath
SERIAL NUMBER 9602-1

The Willie Bivens RB-3 Wreath

The earliest known history of this banjo is absolute. It was purchased brand new on June 27th 1931, by Mr. William Bivens from Carpenters Furniture Store in Rutherfordton NC. Yes friends, I did say "1931", and its serial number is 9602-1! Take a close look at that original Bill of Sale.

NORTH CAROLINA,
RUTHERFORD COUNTY.

Rutherfordton, N. C., June 27, 1931

$138.00

For value, I (or we) promise to pay Carpenter's Furniture Store, or order, the sum of 138.00 Dollars in installments as follows: $25.00 cash balance $2.00 per week each installment to bear interest from date until paid.

The consideration of this obligation is the purchase price of the following articles of personal property this day contracted to be sold me (or us) by said Carpenter's Furniture Store, towit:

1 Gibson Mastertone Banjo $115.00
1 plush lined case 23.00

and it is herein expressly agreed and stipulate that the title to said personal property is and shall remain in said Carpenter's Furniture Store until said purchase price shall have been paid in full. It is further agreed that failure to pay any one of said installments or any part thereof with interest when due shall mature all remaining unpaid installments, or any attempt to remove said property or any part thereof from Spindale N.C. shall mature all remaining unpaid installments, or any attempt to remove said property or any part thereof from .... shall mature all unpaid installments, and Carpenter's Furniture Store, in either event, shall have the right to the immediate possession of said property and every part and parcel thereof.

Witness: .... (Seal)
.... (Seal)

COURTESY GENE KNIGHT

Several Original Bills of Sale, that appear to be dated way too early for their banjos serial number range have come to light in just the past ten years or so, and they always seem to raise questions, and sometimes tempers, but they never cease to completely blow the mind of folks who are dead set in their beliefs of "knowing it all" concerning exactly what year a particular banjo was made and shipped out. They'll say "a 9600 series banjo being made in 1931 is utterly impossible".

Well, I'll have to say that I truly believe a more thorough study of these original dated Bills of Sale, and Gibson's existing shipping ledgers, in just a few years will totally refute all of our previously conceived ideas that say.... a 9500 series banjo should have been made in 1934. I can honestly say that through my own experiences I've found that there is just too much factual evidence and printed proof to simply write these things off as being little oddities.

My good friend and banjo scholar Frank Schoepf has been studying these banjos, and compiling serial numbers, shipping ledgers, dates and original bills of sale for going on 40 years now, way before anyone else even thought much about these types of things, and he has seen and kept meticulous records of numerous original banjos, with their original dated bills of sale, that are completely out of serial order concerning anything we thought we knew for the past 20 years. Concerning what we call serial numbers, Mr. Schoepf feels that these numbers should have never even been given the title "serial number" to begin with. His reason for feeling this way is that he professes that they are not in any particular serial order to begin with. Mr. Schoepf also feels that they would be better understood if they were more accurately called "factory order numbers" for he feels that's exactly what they really were.

I'll have to say that after seeing some of the original shipping ledgers through my good friend's Steve Huber and Walter Carter, I'll have to agree with him, as many of these banjos in the "same serial number range" were shipped out as much as 5 to 10 years apart, and that is definitely not in any serial order.

Mr. Bivens kept and played this particular RB-3 Wreath pattern, for 20 years before selling it to Mack Crow in 1951, for $150.00. Mr. Mack Crow was probably one of the earliest traders in these old original fivestring Gibson banjos, and was well known to have bought and sold several fine old Mastertones throughout the Carolinas in the 40's and 50's. Mr. Crow was one of the first to take notice even at this early time that these old original banjos were far superior to any of the newer banjos for our type of music.

This Wreath pattern RB-3 serial number 9602-1, somehow drifted out of sight and circulation after this time, and absolutely nothing is known of its whereabouts for approximately 16 years, until it showed up in my hometown of Raleigh NC in January of 1967, where it was listed for sale, on a simple student union campus billboard, at N. C. State University for $400.00. This is where it was purchased by my good friend Mr. Gene Knight, who still owns it to this day.

Gene told me that as soon as he got this banjo home after purchasing it, even though he really still didn't know what he had, that he took it completely apart, to clean it, and just to get a better look at what he had bought.

When he removed the trussrod cover he discovered this wonderful piece of "folk art". The original owner, Mr. Willie Bivens of Spindale NC, had taken the time to cut out by hand, little celluloid letters, "Wm. Bivens, Spindale NC", and glued them onto the back side of the trussrod cover with his name and town, and from this information Gene Knight was able to track him down, and received many letters and much information from him over a period of a few years.

Mr. Bivens the original owner was also good friends with Dewitt "Snuffy" Jenkins of Harris NC., who just happened to own two other banjos that are featured in this book.

In Dec. of 1975, Gene Knight the current owner of the banjo was contacted by Mr. Snuffy Jenkins through a letter, asking if he did in fact still own this banjo. It seems Snuffy wanted to purchase this banjo for another of his friends that was looking for one of these fine old banjos.

My good friend Gene Knight has graciously allowed us to copy this letter for the book, and it's full of Snuffy's one of a kind personality. I especially love the line where Snuffy simply calls these extremely rare, desirable Pre War Flathead Gibson Mastertone banjos "Pre War Jobs". That's just hilarious to me!

ORIGINAL WREATH PEGHEAD INLAY.

Columbia, SC.
12-17-75

Mr. Gene Knight,

You don't know me and I don't know you, but I believe you have a banjo that I know who bought it.

Willie Bivens from Rutherfordton bought it when it was new. He wrote me from Titusvill, Ga. and said you own the banjo now.

I have a prewar Gibson but I would like to know if you still have this one Im Talking about?

Is it for sale, if so how much. I know a young banjo player down here that wants a pre-war job like that.

I would appreciate a letter from you if you have time.

Here's hoping Santa Clause is good to you.

Thanks

Dewitt "Snuffy" Jenkins
1014 Sycamore ave.
Columbia, S.C.

Phone 786 7831

LETTER COURTESY GENE KNIGHT

Also note the original envelope from Central Chevrolet Company, of Columbia SC, where Snuffy was employed at the time. He was long retired from playing any fulltime music, and would have only been playing occasionally. Snuffy told an interviewer around this same time that he'd gotten out of the music business years ago "on account of my health", when the interviewer asked what kind of health problems he was having..., Snuffy said... "I was starving to death"....

Snuffy and Gene Knight would have many more conversations regarding this banjo, and Snuffy told Gene in 1976 that this RB-3 Wreath pattern was the first Mastertone banjo that he'd ever seen, back when Willie Bivens bought it brand new. Now Snuffy had no reason whatsoever to lie, and that sure rings true with the "1931" date on the Original Bill of Sale with this banjo, because I know for a fact that Snuffy had seen and played another Mastertone only three years later in 1934.

ORIGINAL FRICTION 5TH PEG AND 5TH STRING NUT.

As said earlier, Gene was able to make contact with the original owner, Mr. Willie Bivens, before his passing, and received this original photo from him featuring this banjo. Gene said that Mr. Bivens had a remarkable memory and dated this photo to April 17th 1932. The players are: Red Owens on Fiddle, Willie Bivens on banjo, and Fred Gossett on Guitar. It seems Mr. Bivens was quite a popular banjo player in the 1930's, and also worked and recorded with J. E. Mainer. He said some of the recordings that he had made with J. E. featuring this banjo were "Lonely Tombs", "Take me back to Colorado", and "Wreck of the old 97". He also said that these records were recorded August 16th, 1939 in Atlanta, on Blue Bird Records.

COURTESY GENE KNIGHT

This rare Wreath pattern RB-3 is standard catalog in every way other than its inlay pattern and, it came from the factory without a Mastertone label. I know of a large batch of original Granada's with the serial number 9526, and 7 out of the 8 banjos that I know of didn't come with a Mastertone label on the inside of the rim, so this is not such a great oddity after all. No one really knows why these banjos left the factory without Mastertone labels, but there's no signs showing that any of them ever had one.

This banjo shows the wear of having been played hard for 70 years. Gene Knight was a busy musician throughout the 70's playing in the popular "New Deal String Band" and also other different band configurations throughout the 80's and up to the present, and has continued to play this banjo exclusively this entire time.

I would like to thank Gene Knight for allowing me to photograph this fine RB-3 Wreath pattern for this book.

ORIGINAL OWNER "WILLIAM (WILLIE) BIVENS" HANDCARVED NAME AND ADDRESS IN TRUE "FOLK ART" LETTERS GLUED INSIDE THE BACK OF THE ORIGINAL TRUSSROD COVER.

Rare original 5 string tensionhoop, and Mastertone block at the 15th fret which is normal on most Wreath pattern banjos.

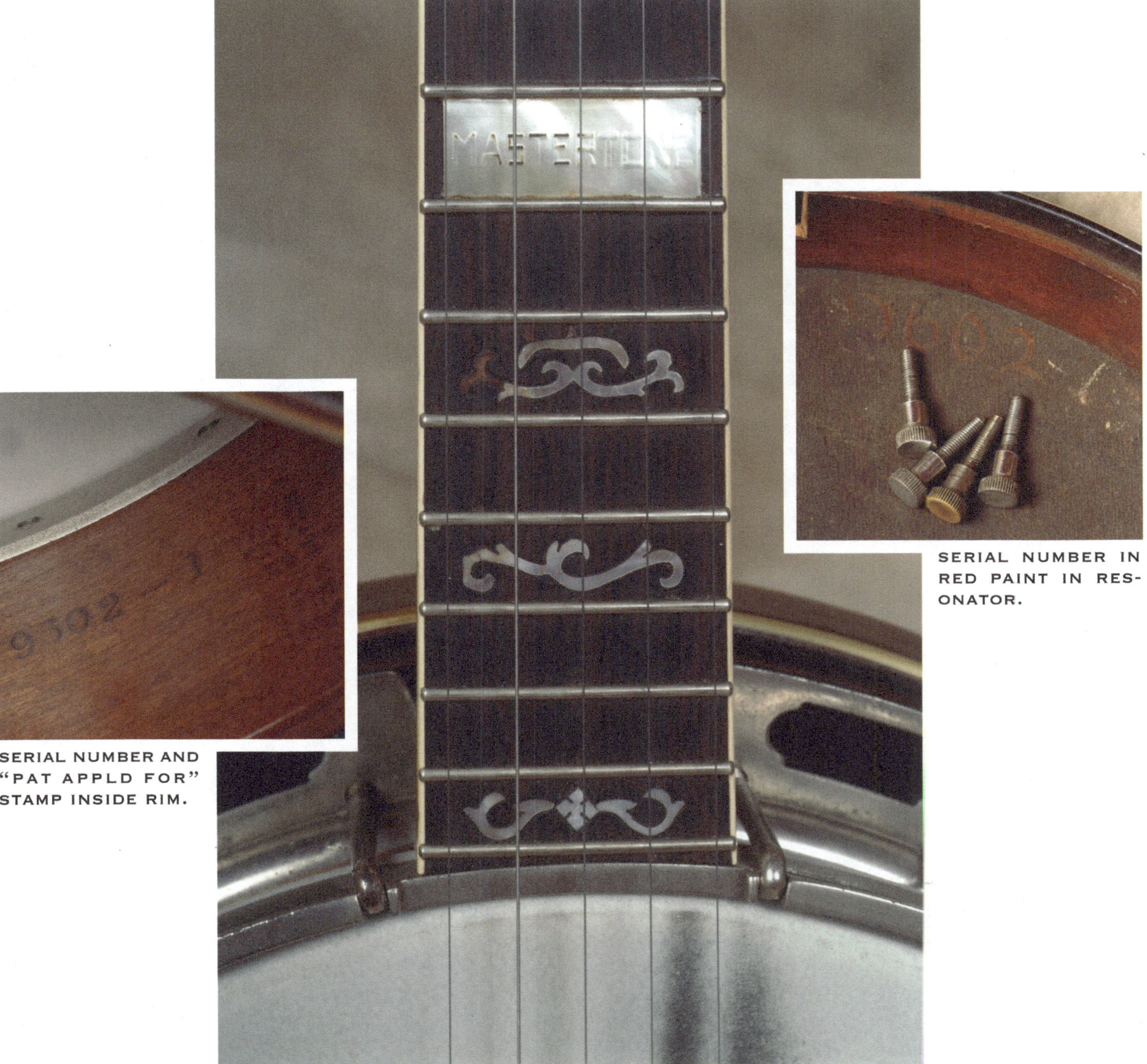

Serial number in red paint in resonator.

Serial number and "Pat Appld For" stamp inside rim.

Provenance:

1. Sold from Carpenters Furniture Store in Rutherfordton NC, on June 27th 1931 to Mr. Willie Bivens for $138.00 including its plush lined case.

2. Willie Bivens kept it 20 years and sold it to Mr. Mack Crow in 1951 for $150.00.

3. Dropped out of sight for some 16 years, and surfaced in Raleigh NC, listed for sale on a campus billboard for $400.00 Jan. 1967.

4. Purchased by the current owner, Mr. Gene Knight, Jan. 1967 for $400.00

The Orval Britton
RB-3
SERIAL NUMBER 177-6

The Orval Britton RB-3

This banjo has had only 2 owners in its long life, Mr. Orval Britton, and Mr. Darrell McCumbers. Mr. Britton claims to have purchased this banjo brand new on December 1st 1934. This date may seem slightly early to many, for this 3 digit serial number range. The exact shipping date on this banjo is not documented for sure, but I would have guessed it to have shipped sometime around 1935, but December of 1934 was only 6 months from the middle of 1935, so this date could in fact be correct. I do know that, what we call "serial numbers" on these banjos were many times shipped in no particular "serial order" whatsoever.

I firmly believe this....and you can mark my words...in the next several years I think "newly discovered information" will surface that will completely blow all of our minds concerning what we think we know about "serial numbers" and also shipping dates on most of these old banjos.

In any event Mr. Britton kept and played this fine banjo for nearly 53 years. It was then purchased from Mr. Britton by my good friend Darrell McCumbers around 1987, and has been in his ownership ever since.

It's a wonderful example of an all original standard RB-3, which believe it or not seem to be harder to find than the coveted Wreath pattern RB-3's. This seems odd, but Steve Huber and I were talking about this very same thing a few years ago, and both of us knew of several original Wreath pattern RB-3's, but very few original five string "Leaves and Bows" inlaid RB-3's, which was the standard factory inlay pattern.

A simple paper label has been affixed inside this banjos rim to commemorate the date Mr. Britton says he purchased this banjo, as can be seen in the photo, and I have no reason to doubt him.

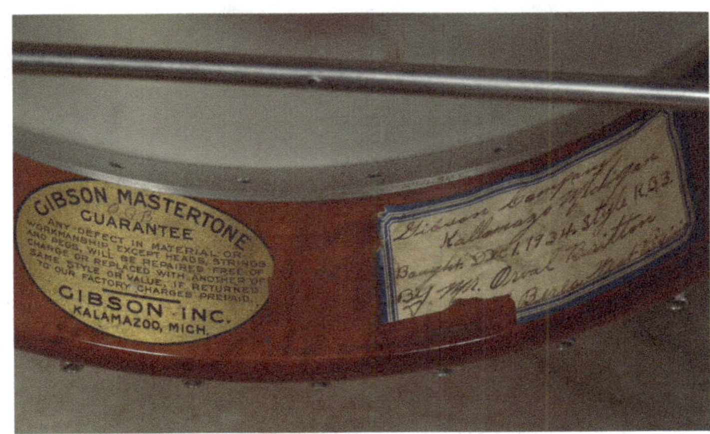

SLIGHTLY CUT MASTERTONE LABEL WITH MR. BRITTON'S "O.G.B." WRITTEN IN, ALSO PAPER LABEL WITH PURCHASE DATE WRITTEN BY ORIGINAL OWNER.

This banjo is standard catalog 1930's RB-3 all the way, featuring all nickel plating, mahogany neck and resonator with white/black/white binding inlaid in rings in the back of the resonator, and a 20 hole high profile flathead tonering. It also still retains its original factory issue, very thin, mid 1930's

STANDARD "LEAVES AND BOWS" FINGERBOARD INLAY, AND PLAIN WHITE BINDING WITH ONLY ONE POSITION MARKER "DOT" AT THE 12TH FRET.

style of frets, and original friction fifth peg. You'll notice the departure of the serial number being in red paint by the heel cut inside the resonator, as the factory changed to using only chalk. The very top of the Mastertone label on this banjo was snipped at the time the tonering was installed. This was a normal practice of the factory at this time, as 99% of the rims that were previously being made up were to be turned into archtop tenor banjos, and this Mastertone label would have been applied before the final cutting of the top of the rim was completed. The 1920's to mid 1930's were really a strong time for banjo sales at Gibson, and they sold many archtop tenors. They would more than likely have been making up several rims at once, before this original Flathead Fivestring RB-3 was even ordered, just trying to stay ahead of the game.

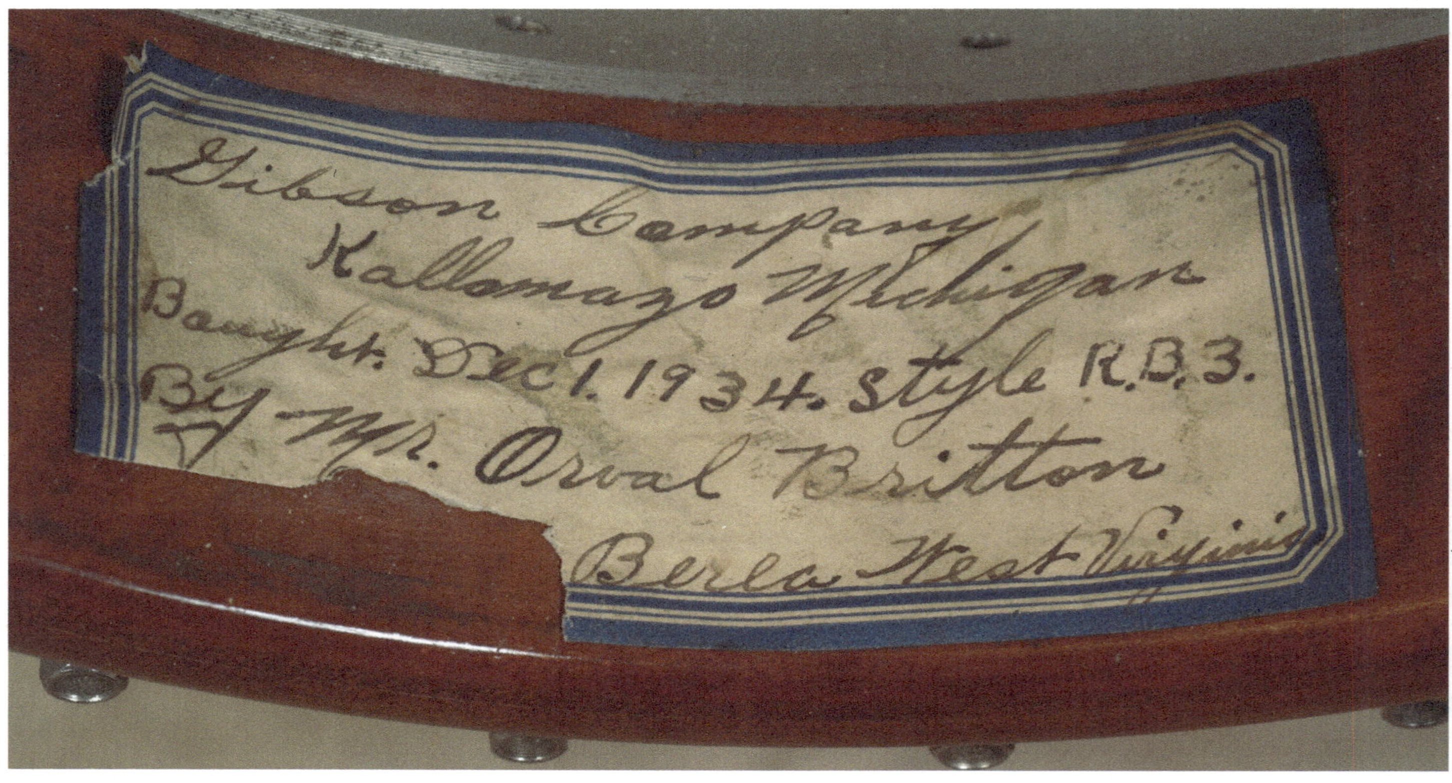

CLOSE UP OF PAPER LABEL.

We have to understand that these pre made rims could have gone on a Tenor, Plectrum, or Fivestring banjo, whatever was ordered first. A few more examples of original factory cut Mastertone labels from this period can be seen in the" Earl Scruggs Granada sn 9584-3", the" Butch Robbins RB-4 sn 9583-1", and also the "Sonny Osborne Granada sn 9584-2" featured in this book.

You'll also see more Original flathead banjos made after approx. 1938 with full uncut Mastertone labels. The tenor banjo craze was dying down by this time, and most of the Original flathead banjos produced during this time were completely started from scratch, after they were ordered, and pre made rims with applied Mastertone labels were more than likely not stock piled very much at all in the late 30's.

This banjo is in very good 100% original condition, with the normal playing wear to the back of the resonator and neck expected from 60 years of playing.

Darrell McCumbers has been a true inspiration to me for many years, both as a collector and a friend, and I would like to thank him publically for allowing me to feature this RB-3 from his fine collection in this book.

PROVENANCE:

1. Reportedly purchased brand new Dec.1st 1934 by Mr. Orval Britton

2. Purchased by its current owner Mr. Darrell Mc-Cumbers circa. 1987

SERIAL NUMBER IN CHALK ONLY.

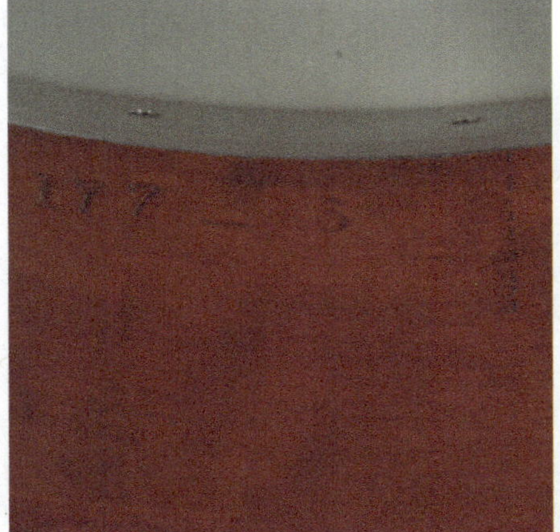

SERIAL NUMBER AND "PAT APPLD FOR" STAMP.

RARE ORIGINAL 5 STRING TENSION HOOP, AND ORIGINAL SMALL FRETS. ALSO SMALL LETTER SIZE IN MASTERTONE BLOCK.

FRICTION 5TH PEG, AND ORIGINAL 5TH STRING NUT.

"The African Queen"
The Rob Tarnow "No Hole" RB-3
SERIAL NUMBER 807-3

The African Queen

This banjo shipped out of the Kalamazoo factory on December 17th 1936, to "H. Polliack, a music store located in Johannesburg South Africa. Yes I did say South Africa! Evidently H. Polliack & Co. LTD. were the premier music store in the whole South African region, and also more than likely the only Gibson dealers in those parts, as I've owned many Pre War Gibson banjos that were originally shipped there, and carried their little yellow and black "Polliack" label. They also had stores in Port Elizabeth, Pretoria, and Capetown. This banjo didn't have a Polliack label, but by simply observing the "Made in USA by Gibson Inc. Kalamazoo Mich." paper label affixed inside the back of the resonator, and also the "Made in USA" stamping into the back of the peghead we would know that this was an exported instrument even if we knew nothing else of its history. This was the Gibson factory's standard procedure on every exported instrument at this time. Luckily for us, this RB-3 banjo is fully listed in the Gibson factory's existing shipping ledgers, and shows exactly where it went and when.

PAPER LABEL AFFIXED TO THE INSIDE OF THE RESONATOR

This African Queen banjo is more than likely one of the very last designated RB-3's to be shipped out of the factory, with its leaving the factory in the middle of the last month of 1936. The style 75 designation came into being in late 1937, and we can see several indicators of this RB-3 being manufactured close to this time even if we didn't know when it actually shipped out. One indicator on this example is the nearly mint condition of all its original metal and nickel plating. By this time, Gibson had worked all the bugs out of their plating process, and also their flange design. They were manufacturing the absolute best plated metal parts of the whole decade that these banjos were produced. The flanges on most examples found from around 1935 and forward tend to be very flat with good plating, unlike many that are found pitted, bubbled, extremely pulled up and ready to crack on several early 1930's examples.

This banjo also has a most interesting history, and I would like to share its story with you. This RB-3 banjo showed up in Johannesburg, South Africa in 1944 in the possession of a fellow by the name of Charlie Macrow. Can you believe that... a guy with an Original Fivestring Flathead with the name Macrow, kind of sounds like "Mack Crow" doesn't it! Where or when Mr. Macrow obtained the banjo is not known. He was a well known teacher of many stringed musical instruments in the Johannesburg area, and taught masses of students during this time. One such pupil was the man I purchased this banjo from, my good friend Mr. Rob Tarnow. He started taking banjo lessons from Mr. Macrow at the age of 12 in 1944. I had Rob write down all the early history he could remember concerning the 63 year period that he owned this banjo, and I'll just quote his exact words...

"Regarding the history of this banjo, the first knowledge that I have is that it was owned by a fellow named Charlie Macrow in the early 1940's. Mr. Macrow was my teacher and taught most of the children of Johannesburg to play nearly all the fretted instruments at this time. Charlie always had a number of spare instruments for pupils who couldn't for any reason bring their own to a lesson. These instruments (of which my banjo was one) were played by anyone who needed one.

PERFECT UNCUT MASTERTONE LABEL, AND EXTREMELY RARE ORIGINAL "NO HOLE" FULL WEIGHT FLATHEAD TONERING.

Charlie was a shrewd business man and was prepared to sell such instruments if the price was right! Where Charlie got this banjo I cannot tell, but I remember he used it for broadcasting when his regular instrument required to be fitted with a new head. (a skin vellum in those days) My mother bought this banjo for me, from Charlie for around 45 pounds, (approx. $40.00 US) towards the end of 1944 or early 1945. I've owned and played it Plectrum style (strung with only four strings) for nearly 64 years now. I Rob Tarnow sold this banjo to Jim Mills October 15th, 2007."

Soon after I purchased this banjo and began telling a few folks about it, I noticed right away that whenever I mentioned my "going to Africa to buy a banjo", everyone automatically imagined "Tarzan, Elephants, Lions and Tigers" and just this whole Hollywood image of some far away land. While it was far away, people don't really stop to think that in the 1930's South Africa was almost like a play ground for wealthy Brits, as it was still under British rule.

It's a beautiful place, and I imagine was a wonderful getaway from the hustle and bustle of most everywhere else in Britain in that era, and many fine Gibson instruments were shipped there in the 1930's, along with several other makes of stringed instruments as well.

The first time I met Rob Tarnow in person, I knew I liked him. He was a tall well spoken gentleman, with the perfect British accent. We spoke of banjo styles and tunes, and I found it most amusing that he had owned this wonderful Original Flathead Fivestring Mastertone Banjo for 63 years, and had never even heard of Earl Scruggs! He had never seen nor heard a banjo played in the three finger style in his native South Africa, and had only been exposed to plectrum and tenor styles which were his passion. He was a very fine Plectrum player and played me a CD of which he and a friend had recorded using this banjo. This original fivestring RB-3 had been void of a fifth string over the entire 63 year period that he owned it, he never used it, but from this recording I could tell that this old RB-3 had been well played during its life, even so with a flat pick and only four strings! I could also tell that it had been very well taken care of.

Check out the photo of Mr. Tarnow at 13 years old, playing this Original Fivestring RB-3 "No Hole" Flathead serial number 807-3 "plectrum style" with a flat pick in 1945 with a friend. Both of these guys are playing original five string banjos, plectrum style with a flat pick!

It also had some of the absolute cleanest metal I've ever seen on any Original Fivestring Flathead. Almost mint condition. The original friction fifth string tuner was left empty and the banjo only had four strings on it, set up with a plectrum bridge. I had known it would be set up this way, so I brought along a fivestring bridge and a new set of strings. I put them on almost immediately, and couldn't wait to play it! The first note I ever hit on it was amazing. I had only played one other banjo like this, and as of this writing there are only three other examples of Original Fivestring RB-3's like this known to exist. The something special I was referring to earlier had to do with this banjos Factory Original "No Hole" Flathead tonering. These "No Hole" rings are a bit of a mystery, as no one really knows why they even exist or were ever made to begin with. It's almost like the guy who drilled the holes in the tonerings didn't show up for work that day or something! It seems that they do show some signs of having been made in batches, as there were several made in the PB-3 batch of serial number 9467. There are at least 5 of them known. Also a few Granada's and style fours were made, and at least three Original RB-3's, including the one featured here. The other Original Fivestring Flathead "No Hole" RB-3 that I had previously played belongs to a good friend of mine on the West Coast, and that banjo was borrowed to record the first few "Bluegrass Album Band" recordings by J. D.

COURTESY THE JIM MILLS COLLECTION

When I arrived in Johannesburg after my grueling straight through 22 hour flight, from Los Angeles to Amsterdam, and then onto South Africa, I was totally worn out, but the next morning I got to meet Rob and his wonderful family, and also this old banjo. When he pulled it out from its original redline case, I knew it was something special. Rob and I had been corresponding with each other for several months concerning this banjo, and I had only seen a few photos of it, so seeing it in real life for the first time was very exciting. The first thing I noticed was its wonderful overall condition. It retained nearly all of its neck and resonator finish which is quite rare on these old banjos as you can see from most of the others featured in this book.

Crowe while he was on the West Coast without his own banjo. This is some of the finest banjo tone known to exist on record, not only in my opinion but in many people's opinion.

COURTESY THE JIM MILLS COLLECTION

J.D. CROWE PLAYING WITH JIMMY MARTIN'S "SUNNY MOUNTAIN BOYS", AND UNKNOWN GIRL. CIRCA 1958.

J. D. Crowe is well known to have played an Original Flathead "No Hole" style 3 banjo for most of his early career, especially on his many recordings with Jimmy Martin throughout the 1950's and 60's. These recordings are regarded as part of the absolute foundations of Bluegrass Music, and are widely considered to be some of the most rock solid, traditional Scruggs style banjo playing, ever to be recorded.

Through the championing of J. D. Crowe alone, these particularly rare style 3 Original Flathead banjos with "No Hole" tonerings have become almost mystical, and are extremely sought after by players and collectors alike for their unique tone characteristics. To my ear they tend to have more of a cutting or penetrating ability than most of the standard 20 hole flathead banjos, and this shows up big time when being played over a microphone. These banjos seem to "stand out in the mix" more so than a lot of other standard 20 hole flathead banjos do, and just have a certain something about them. There again, I can't write it on paper and I can't say it with words, but there is definitely something there. Until recently, I'd never owned one of these rare birds, but after acquiring this "No Hole" RB-3 serial number 807-3, I'll have to say this .... They are absolute "Monsters" of Tone, with power to spare!!!

This particular RB-3 is totally catalog standard in every way and conforms to all factory specs. It is still 100% original overall except for replaced frets. It retains its original deluxe redline case, its friction fifth peg, and both original nuts. All its wood finish is still in remarkable condition as is its original nickel plating. This banjo was never played as a true fivestring for at least 63 years, and therefore never even had fifth string spikes installed. This banjo features the standard "Leaves and Bows" style 3 inlay pattern which seems to be quite rare to find on original fivestrings for sure. Steve Huber and I once had a conversation about how we each knew of more original Wreath pattern RB-3's than original Leaves and Bows standard RB-3's, and this holds true for me today. There is a little oddity concerning this banjos fingerboard scale length also. I'm sure many Banjo scholars have noticed while looking closely at the photo at the end of the fingerboard on this banjo that it seems slightly longer at the very last fret than most original fivestrings tend to.

STANDARD STYLE 3 "LEAVES AND BOWS" INLAY IN DOUBLE CUT PEGHEAD.

Most are cut very close to the last fret and some like the Mack Crow RB-75 have almost nothing there at all. This banjo is totally untouched, and has never been fooled with whatsoever, so I can attest that Gibson wasn't as precise as some may have thought concerning their fingerboard scale measurements, at least on their 1930's and 40's banjos. Another thing to consider is this, a lot of pre war Gibson banjos have been slightly altered over a period of 70 years or more, including having their heels re-shaped and re-cut to better fit their rims, and this can account for some of them being extremely short on the last fret. Then again, I have some that are totally original and were cut this way from the factory.

ORIGINAL FRICTION PEG, AND HIGHLY RARE ORIGINAL LATHE TURNED BONE 5TH STRING NUT.

I have firsthand knowledge of the consecutively serial numbered mate to this RB-3 serial number 807-3, and have seen close up photos of it and the heel cut and scale length at the last fret are identical to this banjo, so I would venture to say that the same guy cut them at the factory. Also please note that the Steve Huber RB-75 listed in this book has a similar length fingerboard scale as this RB-3. So it's easy to conclude that the factory workers in charge of this operation cut them however they felt like at the time basically.

This RB-3 also features a very nice and fiery piece of Brazilian rosewood in its fingerboard, with a lot of black streaks running through it, which I always like to see. There's another small factory oddity concerning this banjo. Remember the serial number inside the resonator in the Posie Roach banjo being rubbed out and another being written in, well this RB-3 had a similar thing going on, except I honestly believe the Gibson factory used an earlier produced, already existing resonator on this banjo. If you look at the chalked numbers inside the resonator, you'll have to look close, but you can make out 9580 in chalk, which was a very large, very well known lot of Original Plectrum Flathead PB-3's mainly found with Wreath patterns, from the early 1930's. Look closer and you can see that a factory worker simply wrote 807-3 over top of it. These things must have gone on there all the time.

LATE STYLE THREE DIGIT SERIAL NUMBER STAMPED INSIDE RIM WITHOUT "PAT APPLD FOR" STAMPING.

Another thing worth mentioning about these rare "exported" pre war Gibson banjos that I've just

INSIDE OF RESONATOR FACTORY CHALKED WITH DOUBLE SERIAL NUMBERS, EXPORT GREEN FELT ON CUTOUT, AND ORIGINAL PAPER "MADE IN THE USA" FACTORY LABEL AFFIXED TO RESONATOR BACK.

recently discovered is something I've not really talked to many people about. I really only began checking into it further after acquiring this RB-3 banjo. In the past few years I'd actually bought and sold several "exported" banjos from this period. I don't know, I'd just had good fortune in finding them. Several were sub Mastertone tenor style 1's, and 11's, and a couple of others, but all were shipped out of the country and four of them were from South Africa. I began to take notice that three of the four had green felt around the cut out in the resonator where nearly every other pre war Gibson banjo I'd seen featured black felt here, also the most interesting feature of these exported banjos was the extra coat of stain and nitrocellulose clear coat that I found applied to the heel cut and also on the tops of the rims of every last one of these banjos. These areas on most of the non export banjos I'd seen for the past 20 years were generally left as bare wood, with maybe only a little stain left on them and that was it. I kind of came to my own conclusion of why this particular practice was performed on all of these exported banjos. After thinking about this for several days, I honestly believe that the Gibson factory of the 1930's really may have not known much about the different climate's of these faraway lands where they were shipping these banjos too, and they simply decided to add a little extra protection to these areas, normally left as bare wood. This they could have thought might help protect them against extreme humid conditions, wood rot, unknown bugs, their long trip on an ocean liner and anything else they could think of at the time. Isn't that cool?

Whatever the reason, it worked, as these fine banjos have survived for over 75 years now in strong, stable, and very playable condition.

This RB-3 is now one of my very favorite banjos to play, and I'm looking extremely forward to recording with it soon. I would like to thank Rob Tarnow, and the whole Tarnow Family for their hospitality, and friendship while there on my short visit. I'll never forget you...

Provenance:

1. Shipped Dec. 17th 1936 to H. Polliack & Co. LTD. in Johannesburg, South Africa
2. Acquired by Charlie Macrow by 1944
3. Purchased by 12 year old Rob Tarnow for 45 pounds= $40.00 US in 1944
4. Purchased by Jim Mills, Oct. 2007 from Mr. Rob Tarnow

CHARLIE MACROW
Johannesburg, South Africa

ONLY A
Gibson
IS GOOD ENOUGH

BILL McMICHAEL
Teacher - Soloist
Newark, Ohio

Every Gibson Instrument has to Run the Gauntlet of Six Inspectors Who are Hard to Please

Every Gibson instrument that leaves this factory has been inspected, checked and re-checked by six individual men whose training of mind, and numerous gauges and other testing devices, enable them to detect the slightest flaw—these men are instructed to throw out any material or instrument that does not come up to Gibson standards. Yes, such inspection is costly, but we are repaid many times over by expressions of satisfaction from thousands of happy Gibson owners.

Check Number One — This man inspects all rough lumber before it is accepted.

Check Number Two — This man inspects all parts in rough shape—and re-checks on number one.

Check Number Three — This man inspects all finished parts—and re-checks on numbers one and two.

Check Number Four — This man inspects all assembled instruments—and re-checks on numbers one, two and three.

Check Number Five — This man inspects all instruments after the finishes have been put on—and re-checks on numbers one, two, three and four.

Check Number Six — This man gives each instrument the final inspection for finish, accuracy, playing ease, tone and volume—and re-checks on numbers one, two, three, four and five.

—is it any wonder that Gibson instruments give more satisfaction and less trouble? And remember —Gibson instruments cost no more!

[46]

UNCLE DAVE MACON
Radio-Records
Nashville, Tenn.

ONLY A
Gibson
IS GOOD ENOUGH

MR. AND MRS. TED BARR
Ft. Wayne, Ind.

GIBSON ENDORSER AND FORMER OWNER OF THE "AFRICAN QUEEN" CHARLIE MACROW FEATURED IN THE 1936 GIBSON "X" CATALOG.

ORIGINAL 5 STRING TENSIONHOOP SHOWING MEDIUM HEIGHT TRANSITIONAL LETTERING IN PEARL MASTERTONE BLOCK.

The Butch Robbins
RB-4

SERIAL NUMBER 9583-1

The Butch Robbins RB-4

This banjo shipped more than likely sometime in the mid 1930's to Texas. Little is known about it until it was acquired by Gary Price of San Antonio TX in 1977. Soon after acquiring it Gary shipped the banjo to George Gruhn in Nashville for an appraisal, where it was inspected by a Gruhn Guitar employee. This employee just happen to be friends with Butch Robbins and told him of this exceptionally fine specimen of an original flathead fivestring RB-4. In 1977 Butch Robbins was on the forefront of Bluegrass banjo playing, working in Bill Monroe's band, The Bluegrass Boys.

THE BLUEGRASS BOYS (BUTCH ROBBINS, SECOND FROM LEFT) CIRCA 1979.

Although he had a good modern banjo at the time, Butch wasn't fully satisfied with its capabilities while being played a long side Kenny Baker's fiddle, and Mr. Monroe's famed 1923 F-5 Gibson mandolin. He knew he wanted a banjo more versatile, a banjo capable of allowing him every expression and variation of tone that he might need to become the best musician he could be. When Butch found this RB-4 serial number 9583-1, he knew he had found his banjo for life.

When George Gruhn saw this banjo's great rarity, which was its complete originality and almost mint condition, he appraised it at a new record high of $6000.00. In 1977 this was an absolutely unheard of evaluation for any type of banjo, and created much talk in the Bluegrass banjo community. Soon after its appraisal, the banjo was shipped back to Gary Price in San Antonio, and not long after Butch contacted Gary to ask if he would consider selling it for the appraised value. An agreement was made that Butch would buy the banjo for $6000.00. Immediately, Butch went to work securing the payment. This was a daunting task to say the least for a working Bluegrass musician in the late 70's. Fortunately, Butch had just recorded a solo album for Rounder Records earlier in the year, and only needed $2500.00 to complete the payment on the banjo. He called Ken Erwin of Rounder Records for a quick loan, and Ken came through with flying colors, and Butch was on his way to getting his dream banjo.

As Butch and his dad drove the many miles to Gary's place in San Antonio Texas to pay for, and also pick up the banjo, he was doubting his decision the whole way, thinking "what in the hell have I done". But when they finally arrived, he opened the case, and was quickly reassured of every reason. Butch's dad even helped to seal his decision, with the fine fatherly advice that seems to come at just the right moment, when he said.... "Son, you'll never have an opportunity to buy another one like this".

Butch told me the banjo was in nearly mint condition, as he was only the third owner, and Gary hadn't had it long, and hadn't altered it in any way. Butch said that after the financial end of the deal was completed and he had a signed "Bill of Sale" in hand, that Gary still had a little reserve about letting the banjo go, but Butch said he didn't hang around long enough to even hear him out, and headed home with his dream banjo. It was all there, skin head, friction fifth peg, original frets, case, and just everything in nearly mint original condition.

I can tell you from my own 20 years of experience trading in these banjos that I've only had one that was that clean, and I may never own another.

These Original Flathead Fivestring Mastertone banjos that can still be found in nearly mint condition, exactly as they left the factory, completely unaltered for over 70 years now, are almost certainly a thing of the past, with fewer surviving with each passing year. Just like this banjo, being newly discovered after lying dormant for many years, most are put back into service and are being played regularly by their new owners. This however, is not a connotation of anything being wrong, as these banjos were definitely made to be played, and I certainly believe in playing them hard, but it would be nice if someone could preserve a few of these nearly mint 100% original examples, if for nothing else but posterity. I've honestly seen only a few Original Flathead Fivestrings in the past 15 years that were in absolutely near mint condition, with their original hang tags, and just everything like new. I've kept up with them, and today these same exact banjos, that were mint only a few years ago, after being played hard for several years by their new owners are merely considered just another good old flathead style 3, 4 or 75, with brass showing on the armrest, scratched up resonators, changed tuners, and a new fret job, planed fingerboards etc. As I said before, I totally agree and understand that they were made to be played, but 99.9% of them are in only very good to average condition today, and probably less than a half dozen examples still exist in nearly mint 100% original condition.

BACK OF RESONATOR HAS SAME SMALL CONCENTRIC RINGS AS THE "SNUFFY JENKINS" RB-4

I fear that in less than 20 years there will be few if any examples left in fine enough condition to be able to say... "That's exactly what a completely original, brand new, 1930's RB-3, 4, 75, or Granada looked like when it left the factory in Kalamazoo MI.".

This same thing has already happened in the Old Master Italian violin world. Only a very minute amount of excellent original examples have been well preserved, and not played almost constantly for over 300 years now, and the majority really show their age and abuse. Some are in such a poor

condition as to be deemed utterly useless to the musician, and are in plain old English, "completely worn out". The world's premiere violin experts and dealers W. E. Hill and Sons decided to bequeath the "Messie" Stradivarius violin to the Ashmolean Museum at Oxford University in 1904, where it still resides today. It is by far the most pristine and original example of a Stradivari violin known in existence, and consequentially has been a wonderful picture into the past for countless enthusiast, builders, and also scientist. It has been examined to the fullest, measured, studied, and copied by nearly every major violin writer, maker, and scientist seeking the absolute pinnacle for over 100 years now. It is said today that nearly every factory made Japanese, German, or US fiddle that has been produced in the past 100 years owes the majority of its look and dimensions to "The Messie Stradivarius".

THIS IS A TYPICAL 1930'S STYLE 4 RESONATOR FROM ANOTHER BANJO, WITH THE CATALOG STANDARD WOOD MARQUETRY INLAID IN CONCENTRIC RINGS.

I think the same can be said concerning the better more modern Bluegrass banjos on the market today, as nearly every successful banjo that has been produced in the past 50 years in some way, conforms to the basic design, construction, and dimensions of a 1930's Gibson Mastertone.

There is a simple reason for this, Old Master Italian violins, and these particular Pre War Gibson Mastertone Banjos will go down in History as having been the absolute best of their type, ever produced. They are the real Benchmark of Quality in the categories of Construction, Design, and Tone.

Back to this RB-4 serial number 9583-1. This banjo like the Snuffy Jenkins RB-4 also features the non typical white-black-white binding inlaid into the back of the resonator. This was not standard catalog on a mid 1930's style 4, it was actually a throwback to the 1920's style 4's which were made of mahogany instead of walnut. The standard catalog specs for this banjo was chrome plating, or "Chromium" as the Gibson catalog described it, with walnut neck and resonator, with wood marquetry inlaid in the back of the resonator. Check out the photo of an example of the standard style 4 wood marquetry in the back of the resonator from another style 4 from the same period. This was the catalog standard.

The Robbins banjo featured here is fitted with both of the two different styles of bindings that were commonly used on these banjos. It has plain white binding on the neck, and the standard (white black white) on the resonator. This is not that strange when one studies very many style 4 banjos from this period. The 1930's style 4's catalog description is as follows...**Wood & Finish** - figured burl walnut finished in rich natural brown. **Neck** - Rosewood fingerboard bound with black and white ivoroid. **Resonator** - Richly figured back, inlaid with rings of colored marguetry. They also came with an upgraded Grover clamshell tailpiece, higher in grade than the plainer Presto of the style 3's, and also Deluxe Grover "two band" tuners another upgrade over the Grover pancakes of the style 3. It seems that style 4's were somewhat of an oddity in that many variations are found in them even in the mid 30's when most other models were pretty consistent. The style 4's were mainly chrome plated, but a few original nickel plated examples exist, and they're usually found with pancake tuners and Presto tailpieces just like a nickel plated style 3. Style 4's are also found with all plain white binding, as well as with the all (white black white) standard type, and sometimes both on the same banjo as with our featured example here. They typically have cut labels on the Original Flathead models that I've encountered, but not always. This banjo is a good example of that also. They all featured either the Hearts and Flowers or Flying Eagle inlays consistently.

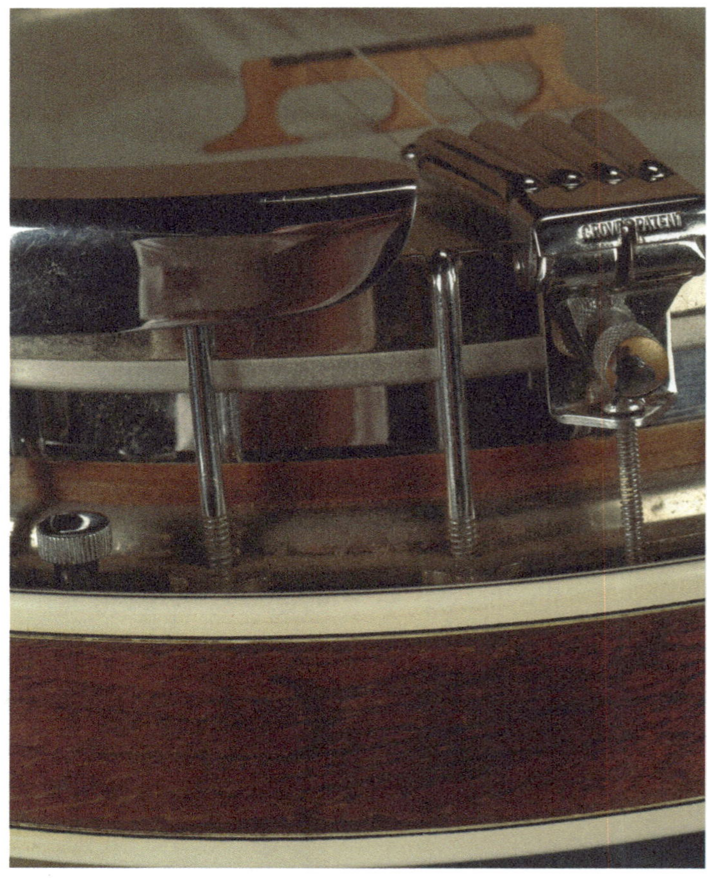

W/B/W BINDING ON RESONATOR, AND STANDARD CHROME PLATED METAL, ALSO RARE ORIGINAL FACTORY 5 STRING GIBSON BRIDGE.

When Butch started playing this banjo all over the world in 1977, he had the foresight to get many important and now completely unobtainable autographs (due to most being deceased) which only adds greatly to this banjos historical importance. He was smart enough to get the absolute forefathers of the three finger style early on..Snuffy Jenkins, Earl Scruggs and Don Reno. He also got another who many consider the father of the melodic style Mr. Bill Keith. They can clearly be seen inside of the resonator photo.

This is a very fine example of an RB- 4 Original Flathead, and I would like to thank Butch again for allowing us to photograph it for this book.

DOUBLE CUT PEGHEAD DESIGN FEATURING THE "HEARTS AND FLOWERS" INLAY PATTERN, AND NOTICE THE TOP OF THE "G" ON GIBSON ALMOST RUNS OFF THE PEGHEAD, THIS IS COMMONLY SEEN ON THIS PATTERN.

PROVENANCE:

1. Shipped from the factory circa mid 1930's, and purchased by its unknown original owner
2. Purchased by Gary Price in 1977
3. Purchased by Butch Robbins in 1977, current owner

RARE DOUBLE STAMPED SERIAL NUMBER 9583, ONE DIGIT FROM EARLS GRANADA 9584! ALSO "PAT APPLD FOR" STAMP.

RARE ORIGINAL 5 STRING TENSION HOOP, AND SMALL LETTERING IN MASTERTONE BLOCK.

THE INSIDE OF THE RESONATOR HAS BEEN SIGNED BY MANY PIONEERS OF THE THREE FINGERED STYLE OF BANJO.

UNPOLISHED DULL UNDERSIDE TO ORIGINAL 1 PC CHROME FLANGE, AND CHROME L BRACKETS.

SLIGHTLY CUT ORIGINAL MASTERTONE LABEL.

The Snuffy Jenkins RB-4

SERIAL NUMBER 9639-1

The Snuffy Jenkins RB-4

The first record we have of this banjo existing is, that it was shipped out of the factory April 5th 1937. This factual information was just recently revealed to me. I had previously only had passed down verbal information that this banjo had been purchased brand new from Alexander Music House in SC in 1935. I even printed this same wrong information in several articles concerning this banjo in the past few years. There again the original Gibson shipping ledgers don't lie, even though it seems that this banjo shipped a little later than what we may think for its serial number range. This further shows how Gibson banjo serial numbers after about 1929 are totally unreliable when used to date exactly when a certain banjo may have left the factory. In reality they should not be called serial numbers at all because they don't follow any sort of serial pattern 100% of the time.

PHOTO: GIL GOLIN

SNUFFY PERFORMING WITH FLATT & SCRUGGS IN 1968, PLAYING BOTH RB-GRANADA 9584-3, AND RB-4 9639-1. SNUFFY OWNED BOTH OF THESE BANJOS IN 1940.

It does still seem that the first owner apparently bought this banjo new in 1937 for $175.00, kept it for 3 years, got married, got into debt, and had to pawn it for around $40.00. This is the story that was relayed by the Spartanburg SC pawnshop owner, when DeWitt "Snuffy" Jenkins walked into his pawnshop one day in 1940, and inquired about this banjo. The $175.00 conforms to the prices of the day. According to the 1935 Gibson catalog, the style RB-4 banjo retailed for $150.00, and the deluxe, plush lined, faultless case that it came in sold for $22.00. This banjo also came equipped with a factory headguard, which retailed for $3.00. The ship date doesn't conform to the 1937 catalog availability, as the style 3, 4, Granada and all other standard pot construction banjos had been discontinued, but several style 4's, Granada's, and other supposed discontinued models continued to ship through part of 1937. These banjos could have been ordered in late 1936, we don't know, but again the shipping ledgers don't lie.

The pawnshop owner said he wanted $40.00 for the instrument, and Snuffy knew the banjo was a bargain, even at that time, in the poverty stricken south. Although Snuffy didn't need it, he already had a great banjo at home, RB-Granada Sn 9584-3, the banjo that Earl Scruggs would later make famous, he bought this RB-4 Sn 9639-1 anyway, and proceeded home to Columbia SC. After comparing what would become two of the most famous banjos in the world, Snuffy found this new RB-4 more to his liking, and sold the Granada to a then teenaged Don Reno for $90.00. Reno would later trade the Granada in 1949 to Earl Scruggs, who played, and recorded with it for the rest of his career. Not only was Snuffy an early pioneer of the three finger picking style of North Carolina, he was also an important influence on both Scruggs, Reno, and countless others.

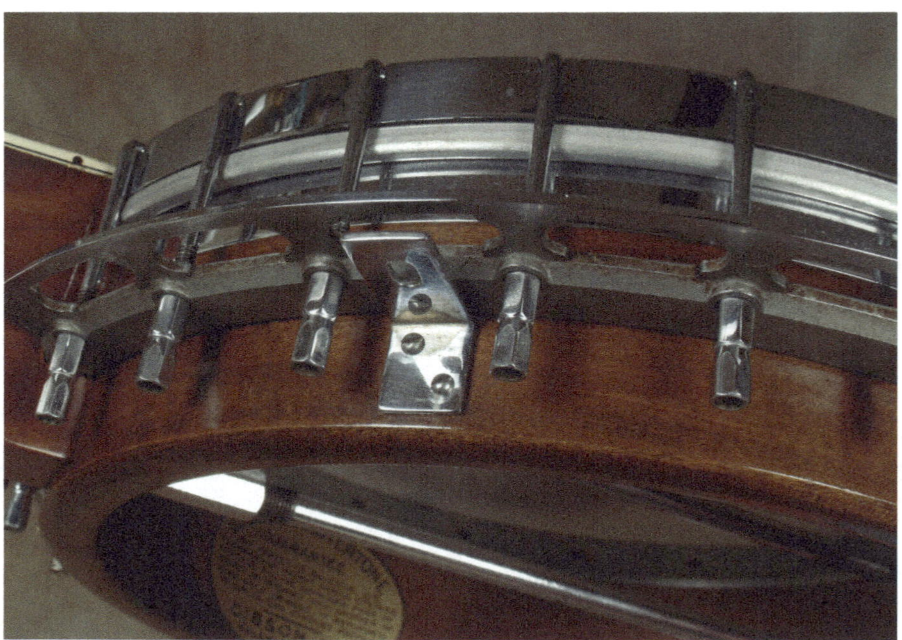

PHOTO SHOWS UNPOLISHED DULL UNDERSIDE OF ORIGINAL CHROME PLATED 1 PC FLANGE.

The fact that Snuffy was performing with both the Granada first, and then the RB-4, on personal appearances in their area, and being heard by them on the radio, while they were both little boys, is the main reason, as far as I'm concerned, that both Reno and Scruggs eventually searched out, and found an original Fivestring Flathead Gibson Mastertone to play throughout their careers. It has been documented many times that both of these young boys had seen, and heard Snuffy by the 1930's at live performances, and had also been listening to him over WBT radio, in Charlotte NC, and later WIS radio, in Columbia SC. This would have been from 1934 on. The main reason I think they were so interested in the type of banjo that Snuffy played, is because Snuffy would have sounded completely different when compared to any of their earliest influences, such as Smith Hammett, and Rex Brooks, and Mack Woolbright. These men were mainly relatives and friends, performing at family gatherings, and dances, etc, on the simple open back type of banjos, common to the rural amateur banjo player of that time. These men also were still playing with only their finger nails and no picks. I have to believe that these 2 boys saw Snuffy as a professional musician, with a sponsor on a large radio station, trying to make a living at something other than farming, and you can't tell me they didn't both take notice of what type of banjo he was picking. It was a big, shiny, and loud, one piece flange, 1930's "Flathead Fivestring Gibson Mastertone" with pearl inlay all over the fingerboard. In the mid to late 30's when these boys were first seeing Snuffy, these newer Gibson Mastertone Banjos must have looked and sounded absolutely unbelievable, when compared to the tiny little, plain, dot and star inlaid open back banjos they were used to seeing.

Snuffy was, as far as anyone can trace, the first to play the three finger style on radio. He's also reported to be one of the first to make use of metal fingerpicks. Snuffy learned the three finger style directly from both Smith Hammett, and Rex Brooks, the two men most claim to be the earliest proponents of the style. Both of these men reportedly played with only a thumbpick and fingernails, or just their fingernails. Snuffy claimed also to have learned the three-finger style directly from them, but needed to be heard over the other instruments when he began playing on radio broadcast, and the metal picks on both fingers, along with a thumbpick did the job. Snuffy never claimed to have taught Scruggs or Reno anything, but admits whenever he performed live, near the homeplace of either one, they would almost always show up, and spend some time together backstage. The fact remains that Snuffy was nearly 20 years older than either of these two boys, who at the time would have been approximately 10 to 14 years old. It's almost unimaginable that they didn't look up to him just a little, as a musician. Snuffy had been playing the three- finger style of banjo since 1927, and heard on the two most listened to radio broadcast in the area since 1934. Therefore I see this man, Snuffy Jenkins, as one of the most important men in history concerning the creation of bluegrass banjo playing as we know it today. As for these two banjos, Snuffys RB-4 sn 9639-1, and Earls Scruggs Granada sn 9584-3, both of which Snuffy Jenkins owned at the same time in 1940, I see as two of the most important Flathead Fivestring Gibson banjos in existence, as far as the history of bluegrass is concerned.

PHOTO SHOWING, W/B/W BINDING, SNUFFY'S ORIGINAL EBONY AND BONE TOP BRIDGE, CHROME PLATED METAL, AND ORIGINAL GROVER CLAMSHELL TAILPIECE.

Some may say that Earl Scruggs is the only reason Gibson banjos are collectable today, and with all due respect I would surely agree that he's done more to promote these particular banjos, and the banjo in general, than anyone else will likely ever do again in history, but everything has to start somewhere, and I consider Snuffy Jenkins, playing these two banjos, the nucleus, seed, or foundation of why we all want an Original Pre War Flathead Mastertone banjo, or some form of replica, either to play, or collect.

Being from North Carolina myself, I've kept track of most of the first generation 3 finger style players of NC, and also their earliest influences. Snuffy Jenkins was without a doubt the most influential player of the late 1930's and early 40's, mainly because of radio broadcast. This is of course before Earl Scruggs began his professional career in 1945, playing with Bill Monroe on the Grand Ole Opry. Pioneers such as Don Reno, Earl Scruggs, Johnny Whisnant, Rudy Lyle, Ralph Stanley, Jim Smoke, and Hoke Jenkins, all site Snuffy Jenkins in print, among their earliest of influences. How then can this true pioneer of the three finger roll ever be denied the utmost stature! Snuffy simply never touted these facts in public or print very much, but continued to record, and perform with this RB-4 Sn 9639-1 for half a century, from 1940 until his death in 1990. Today he's mainly remembered as a good comedian, and a somewhat rough banjo player from the few recordings that have survived. The shame of the whole situation is that Snuffy never got to record a great deal while in his prime as a player in the 1930's and 40's, as the war came along and restricted all recording basically. Nothing from this era of his prime other than a poor recording from 1941 exist today. If you get a chance listen to "Gonna Lay Down my Old Guitar" from the early 40's in D tuning. It's some of the finest banjo playing to be found anywhere, and I can get a small

COURTESY THE JIM MILLS COLLECTION

glimpse into just why Reno spoke so passionately about Snuffy's playing from the 1930's and 40's. It's a real shame that he has to be judged today by these recordings that were made several years after his playing prime, when he had all but quit playing, and was merely half the player he had been in his 20's and 30's. Don Reno said in an interview that Snuffy was playing tunes like "Dear Old Dixie", "Sally Ann", "Sally Goodwin", and "Cumberland Gap" in the 1930's and absolutely burning them up! He said it sounded remarkably similar to the recordings Scruggs would make of these same songs over 20 years later. This was before the comedy routines became his main focus, and his banjo playing was most important to him. The circa 1939 photo of Snuffy featured here is one of many that I received from the family when I purchased the banjo, and you can see he is playing the RB-Granada serial number 9584-3, that Earl Scruggs would later make famous, but look how Snuffy is dressed, a white dress shirt and tie, not in his comedy garb, and look at that right hand man!! It just doesn't get any better than that! I'll bet Snuffy was a bad man in 1939!

Snuffys old RB-4 has survived in remarkable condition, having been owned for 64 years by only one family. It is still unbelievably 100% original. It features an uncut Mastertone label, 20 hole flathead tonering, chrome plating, all original wood finish, factory headguard, clamshell tailpiece, and Flying Eagle inlay. This and a few other style 4 banjos from this period have the earlier 1920's style white/black/white concentric rings inlaid in the back of the resonator rather than the standard wood marquetry. It is a very thin, white / black / white type of binding. The standard catalog style 4 of the mid 1930's period had intricate wood marquetry rings inlaid in the back of the resonator. Butch Robbins RB-4, also featured in this book, has the same type binding as Snuffys. By the way, Butch Robbins recently told me that he installed the very first plastic head ever put on Snuffys banjo in 1969, as he

STANDARD DOUBLE CUT PEGHEAD DESIGN, WITH "FLYING EAGLE" INLAY PATTERN.

PHOTO SHOWS SMALLER FACTORY ORIGINAL W/B/W CONCENTRIC RINGS IN BACK OF RESONATOR, AND GROOVE WORN IN HEEL AREA FROM SNUFFY'S OWN HAND DURING COMEDY SKITS.

and Snuffy had become good friends by then, and the old calfskin head that was on it was busted and needed replacing.

The neck on this RB-4 Sn 9639-1 is of a wonderful size and very playable. This is the main reason why I believe Snuffy chose this banjo over RB-Granada Sn 9584-3 in 1940. I know from reliable reports that Earl cut the neck down on the Granada with a wood rasp, implying it had a pretty big neck. The neck and resonator of this RB-4 are of very fine walnut, and have quite a bit of wear to the finish on the back of the neck, and a small amount on the resonator. It has a worn spot on the heel of the neck, where Snuffys fingers shaped a groove into the wood, where he held it while performing his comedy routines. He would frequently throw it over his right shoulder and let it hang down while doing his comedy skit. It's a sheer wonder that the neck's heel or peghead wasn't cracked or broken in all the time he performed with it for nearly 50 years. It still retains its original fifth string nut, and friction peg, as well as the other nut. This banjo is so original that it's never even had fifth string spikes installed. Snuffy liked to play in open keys and would usually just tune up when necessary. The original case, although very worn, and the original wrench are still with the banjo. Snuffys personalized strap, and many photos documenting a long career from the 1930's through the 80's were also included, when the author purchased this banjo from the Jenkins family in 2004. It had been in the Jenkins family for 64 years, and had never been offered for sale. Outside of replaced frets, and a new head, it's as original as the day it left the factory in Kalamazoo MI.

I recently recorded with this banjo on my latest CD "Hide Head Blues", on Sugar Hill Records, and I'll have to say that it's absolutely the loudest flathead I've ever played, and also has a very powerful tone.

FACTORY ORIGINAL LATHE TURNED HIGH FIFTH STRING NUT, FRICTION PEG, AND W/B/W STANDARD STYLE 4 BINDING.

The Snuffy Jenkins RB-4 is undoubtedly one of the most important artifacts in the early history of Bluegrass music, as well as pioneering the whole 3 finger style of playing in North Carolina. In my humble opinion, Earl Scruggs should no doubt hold the title 'The Father of the three fingered style", but Snuffy Jenkins should be considered the "Granddaddy of it all"!

This RB-4 banjo is currently on loan to the Country Music Hall of Fame, and is featured in the "Pioneers of Country Music" exhibit. It's only a few yards down the hall from Bill Monroe's famed 1923 Lloyd Loar F-5 mandolin also on exhibit there. Go see them both if you get the chance.

COURTESY THE JIM MILLS COLLECTION

SNUFFY JENKINS IN FULL COMEDIAN DRESS, PLAYING RB-4 SERIAL NUMBER 9639-1 CIRCA-1940'S.

PHOTO SHOWS UNPOLISHED INNER FACE OF ORIGINAL CHROME FLATHEAD TONERING, SERIAL NUMBER STAMP, "PAT. APPLD FOR" STAMP, AND LONG NUT ON BOTTOM COORDINATOR ROD, WHICH DISAPPEARED SOON AFTER THIS TIME.

SERIAL NUMBER IN CHALK ONLY, AND YOU CAN SEE WHERE ANOTHER NUMBER WAS RUBBED OUT AT THE FACTORY, BY THE TIME THIS BANJO SHIPPED OUT IN THE MIDDLE OF 1937, IT SEEMS THEY HAD ABANDONED USING RED PAINT ALTOGETHER ON SERIAL NUMBERS.

PERFECT MASTERTONE LABEL.

Provenance:

1. Shipped from the factory April 5th 1937 to Houk Music Company
2. Unknown first owner
3. Pawnshop owner in Spartanburg SC, ca. 1940
4. Dewitt "Snuffy" Jenkins, ca. 1940
5. Descended into Jenkins family at Snuffys passing 1990
6. On loan to The South Carolina Country Music Hall of Fame 1995-2004
7. Purchased from Jenkins Family by Jim Mills, 2004
8. On loan to The Country Music Hall of Fame, on exhibit since 2005 and currently still there.

HIGHLY RARE ORIGINAL CHROME PLATED 5 STRING TENSION HOOP.

The Sonny Osborne RB-Granada

SERIAL NUMBER 9584-2

The Sonny Osborne RB-Granada

The first record we have of this banjo is that it is believed to have been purchased brand new by Scotty Wiseman of the recording group "Lulu Belle and Scotty" sometime around 1934 or 35. The original Gibson factory shipping ledgers that still exist today only go back to 1936 and forward, so there is no way to prove beyond a shadow of a doubt exactly where or when it shipped originally, but it seems very likely that it was shipped to Chicago, as Scotty was working there; on radio station WLS at that time. The WLS Barn dance was a very successful radio program at this time, and was really considered the only competitor to the Grand Ole Opry in Nashville. The publicity photo featured here of Lulu Belle and Scotty from the 1930's, shows Scotty playing an original fivestring Flathead RB-Granada, with Hearts and Flowers inlay, and it is thought to be this very banjo . He was well known for taking the resonator off the banjo while playing, to allow a more mellow old time sound. Scotty was also well known for playing Gibson Mastertone banjos, and owned at least 2 more besides this one. It's not known whether he was a Gibson endorser at this time, as he is not pictured in any Gibson catalog that I am aware of, but is pictured later in a1940's publicity photo, playing an RB-18 top tension model. I also have knowledge of an original factory shipping ledger written after 1937 that shows him sending in another RB-Granada to the Kalamazoo Plant for repair, that is not serial number 9584-2, the RB- Granada featured here. Scotty evidently sold RB-Granada sn 9584-2 at some point, and from there we kind of lose track of it for many years until it shows up again in the hands of world renowned Vintage instrument dealer George Gruhn in the mid 1970's. It didn't stay there long, as Tom McKinney of Asheville NC soon purchased it from Gruhn. Tom held onto it for a while and when The Osborne Brothers played a show in nearby Knoxville TN, he invited them back to his home for dinner, and also to spend the night. After arriving at his home, Tom began showing several banjos to Sonny. Sonny has told me many times that he really didn't think Granada serial number 9584-2 was anything very special at first. He said that right in the middle of their late night dinner, something struck him, he excused himself, and he went back into the living room and began playing it again. He

Sincere Best Wishes
Lulu Belle & Scotty

COURTESY THE JIM MILLS COLLECTION

LULU BELLE AND SCOTTY KNOWN AS "THE SWEETHEARTS OF COUNTRY MUSIC" WERE ONE OF THE MAJOR COUNTRY MUSIC ACTS OF THE 1930'S AND 1940'S.

said it was like a light came on in a dark room. He absolutely could not put it down, and realized then and there what he had been missing all these years in other banjos. It was the absolute sweetest tone he'd ever heard, and he knew he must have it at all cost! Sonny played the banjo from around midnight till 4:00am. The next morning he informed Tom that he wasn't leaving without this banjo! Tom didn't really care to part with the banjo, but Sonny was very adamant about it. He and Tom began negotiations concerning what would later become known as "a true landmark sale" in this type of banjo. On New Year's Day 1978, Sonny Osborne paid $5000.00 for this RB-Granada banjo! It was the second highest price ever paid, for any type of banjo, known at that time. This high profile sale helped to set a new standard for all original flathead fivestring Mastertones to follow for many years to come. Not only was this sale highly visible in the Bluegrass banjo world, its extreme high price also raised the awareness of every dealer, player, and collector, as to the infinite, and extreme rarity of these instruments. It almost singlehandedly raised the bar on the entire Pre War Gibson banjo market, and helped these particular banjos reach the high status that they still enjoy today. Put this into perspective..at this time in America, a brand new high performance Z-28 Chevy Camaro, or Mach-1 Ford Mustang could be purchased for approximately the same price as Sonny paid for this banjo. Compare that to the top high performance auto prices of today and you'll come to a fast conclusion of just how much money this was at that time. This one sale opened many eyes, mainly because of Sonny's high profile in the business, and also his outgoing personality and authority in the banjo world. Also he was very open to talking about these banjos, and therefore helped greatly to gain these banjos the high level of respect, which they have held every since. Sonny has said in print many times that this banjo gave him a new lease on his career, and that it really inspired him to play again. The Osborne Brothers as a band, had accomplished nearly everything a Bluegrass Band could ever dream of by 1977, they'd played for Presidents, been members of the Grand Ole Opry for 13 years, they'd had hit records, and recorded an all time classic with "Rocky Top" which would later become the Tennessee State Song, along with many other high accolades throughout there long career. There really wasn't much they had left to conquer, or to look forward too as a band. Sonny said that when he purchased this banjo it made him really

COURTESY THE JIM MILLS COLLECTION

THE OSBORNE BROTHERS, BOBBY AND SONNY.

PEGHEAD SHOWING "HEARTS AND FLOWERS" INLAY PATTERN, AND ORIGINAL SOLID MOTHER OF PEARL TUNER BUTTONS.

want to play again, and renewed his love for the banjo. It added many years to a career that was already fully satisfying.

I for one can say it's truly a great banjo, as I've had the honor to be asked by Sonny to play it on several occasions both on and off stage, and it really has the ability to give whatever you ask of it. Throughout the late 1980's and early 90's, when I was working in Doyle Lawson's group Quicksilver, I got the opportunity to see Sonny nearly every weekend throughout the summer, as we played most of the same festivals, and I remember several times he would have just put on a new bridge, or changed something setup wise, and he would say "Mills play this thing on your next set, I want to see what it sounds like". This of course was a great honor for me, and I can say with all honesty that RB-Granada sn 9584-2 has highs, lows, sustain, crack, and anything else you can think of. Although it's not the loudest banjo I've ever played, it has the most desirable quality that you could ever hope for in a banjo... the ability to cut straight through, and penetrate a microphone, and transfer its natural tone beautifully both on stage and in the studio.

THE AUTHOR AND THE SONNY OSBORNE RB-GRANADA

COURTESY THE JIM MILLS COLLECTION

I've included a photo of me playing this RB-Granada serial number 9584-2 several years ago, someone snapped a quick photo of me as I was going on stage with the legendary late fiddler, Robert "Chubby" Wise. You can see "Sonny" on the strap if you look close, and also brother Bobby Osborne in the background. The banjo still had its original neck installed at this time, and was an absolute dream to play.

When Sonny first obtained this banjo it was in very clean condition and 100% original in every way except for a replaced flange, which is very common because they tend to break very easily. Many years later he removed the original 5 string neck for fear of damage, and had Mr. Frank Neat build him an exact replica of the original neck, which he played until recently. He also replaced the original pearl button, 2 band Grover tuners that came on these banjos with the smaller Grover pancake tuners, as they work much smoother, and are easier to change strings on in a constant working environment. He then replaced the original Grover clamshell tailpiece with a Presto, because they're also easier to change strings on when one breaks on stage. However, when I called Sonny and told him of my idea for this book, and also of my interest in having all the banjos photographed in as close to fully original condition as possible, he was gracious enough to put this fine banjo back to its original specs for this photo shoot, and I thank him very much for it.

BACK OF PEGHEAD SHOWS ORIGINAL "TWO BAND" GROVER TUNERS, AND SOLID MAPLE PEGHEAD WOOD OVERLAY, UNIQUE TO GRANADA'S. THIS IS BELIEVED TO BETTER CONTINUE THE GRAIN PATTERN OF THE NICER CURLY MAPLE, WHERE NO GLUED ON EARS WOULD EVER BE SEEN.

This RB-Granada banjo is serial number 9584-2. The serial number series "9584" itself has become almost legendary in the past several years. There are only 5 banjos known to have been produced with this serial number, 9584-1, 9584-2, 9584-3, 9584-4, and 9584-5. All of these banjos were original flathead fivestring RB-Granada's, with Hearts and Flower inlay, except for 9584-4, which was shipped out much later than the rest of this batch of RB-Granada's as a TB-18.

The most famous of this serial number batch however is.. RB-Granada 9584-3, featured in the pages of this book, which is Earl Scruggs' famous Granada that he's played for most of his career, making the remainder in this serial number batch all brethren, and therefore gaining them an almost Royal like status, and a most respectful following among Pre War Gibson banjo enthusiasts. I count myself as one of the fortunate few who have seen and played them all.

BACK OF RESONATOR SHOWING WEAR AND FACTORY "GRANADA" SUNBURST FINISH.

To show just how little information in general was available on these banjos when Sonny purchased it in 1978, neither he nor Tom McKinney had any idea whatsoever that this banjo was a consecutive serial numbered mate to the Scruggs' Granada!! This can be attributed to so little accurate information being documented by anyone on a regular basis yet. Sonny continued to play and record with this banjo until 2005, when he underwent surgery for a torn rotator cuff in his left shoulder, and has since retired from the Osborne Brothers Band. He does however keep busy doing a number of banjo workshops in and around Nashville, and also abroad throughout the year. He also markets a very successful line of new banjos known as "The Chief", Sonny's nickname, which are replicas of this wonderful RB-Granada serial number 9584-2. They are built in conjunction with Frank Neat, and are very fine banjos also.

This RB-Granada is in a fine state of preservation, considering its life. Sonny was pretty hard on this banjo early on, playing it so much throughout the year. Performing on an instrument for such a long period of time, in the heat of summer, combined with the humidity and unpredictable weather at outdoor Bluegrass Festivals, and also traveling so many miles per year, by both bus, and plane will undoubtedly take its toll on anything after so many years. All the Granada's in this batch feature Hearts and Flowers inlay which is absolutely a thing of beauty in itself. This banjo represents the original 5 string H&F inlay pattern as it came from the factory new. Earl Scruggs had the two inlays added to his neck at the 1st and 15th frets at a later date, and this pattern has been copied so many times by modern banjo builders, that the more simplistic but beautiful original 5 string 1930's factory Hearts and Flowers inlay pattern is almost unknown to all but the most serious of banjo students. Some tenor and plectrum Granada's and style 4's featured these extra H&F inlays originally from the factory, but most feature the more simplistic H&F pattern shown on this banjo. This is the way all of the RB-Granada's in this serial number batch came originally from the factory.

As I said, I have been fortunate enough to have played all four of the original RB-Granada's in this serial number series, and I'll have to say that this is one great banjo.

Thank you Sonny, for the inspiration your playing on this great banjo has given us through the years over your long and successful career.

PROVENANCE:

1. Reportedly ordered new by Scotty Wiseman of "Lulu Belle and Scotty" fame circa. Mid 1930's.

2. Sells a few more times in 40 year period to un known persons

3. Turns up in the possession of George Gruhn in the mid 1970's

4 Sold to Tom McKinney circa. 1975

5. Sold to Sonny Osborne New Years Day 1978 for $5000.00

SERIAL NUMBER PAINTED IN RESONATOR IN STANDARD RED PAINT.

SLIGHTLY CUT MASTERTONE LABEL LIKE ALL THE OTHERS IN THIS BATCH.

ORIGINAL WHITE/BLACK/WHITE BINDING ON RESONATOR, AND ENGRAVED ARMREST.

ORIGINAL BRASS, (MOST WERE MADE OF POT METAL), GRANADA 5 STRING TENSIONHOOP, AND PEARL MASTERTONE BLOCK SHOWING THE TYPICAL SMALL LETTERING FROM THIS PERIOD.

STANDARD GRANADA ENGRAVING PATTERN ON TENSION HOOP.

The Earl Scruggs RB-Granada

SERIAL NUMBER 9584-3

The Earl Scruggs RB-Granada

The first documentation of any that we have on this banjo comes from a letter dated June 1934 by Fisher Hendley. The banjo is believed to have been ordered from the factory early in 1934, and purchased brand new by Mr. Fisher Hendley, from a dealer named Jim Graves. In addition to being the local barber of Wadesboro North Carolina, it seems Mr. Graves was the only authorized Gibson instruments dealer in this rural part of North Carolina at this time. I obtained this information directly from Buck Wheless, son of Dewitt Wheless, another North Carolina banjo player working on station WBT, and also one of Fisher Hendley's best friends. Mr. Buck Wheless relayed this story to me of how his father Dewitt Wheless, and Mr. Hendley each ordered, and then picked up together, several months later, in the middle of 1934, their own original flathead fivestring RB-Granada's, together on the same day from this Wadesboro Barbershop! When Mr. Wheless began to recount this event to me, completely unprompted, and very nonchalantly, it was very evident to me that he'd heard this story all his life from his father. To say the least, I was completely overwhelmed.

J. W. FINCHER
Manager for
The Carolinas

239 N. Tryon St.
P. O. Box 1317
Telephone 5716

CRAZY WATER CRYSTALS CO.
Mayfair Hotel Bldg.,
CHARLOTTE, N. C.

June.18.1934.

Mr.Stephen N.Crump,
Waco,Texas.
My Dear Cousin:

Sometime ago I recieved your most interesting letter,and I am just ashamed that I haven't answered it sooner.But I have been up to my neck in work.This broadcasting keeps me quite busy,and too we get about three thousand pieces of fan mail each week.I had the station announcer to read your letter over the radio,and since that time I have had lots of people most of them your old acquaintances to either telephone,or write in and ask about you.I hope you heard the broadcast.

Marsh Hendley lives in Gaffeney,S.C.Ab Hendley,lives at Cedar Hill at the old John Greene place.Tink Hendley lives at the old home place where he was reared.I haven't seen your mother Cousin Victoria in quite awhile. When I lived in Albemarle she use to visit me sometimes for two weeks at a time.She is a dear sweet lady,and always seemed like a mother to me. And I dearly love her.I am going to see her as soon as I can possibly do so.I hope you will be able to pay us a visit in the near future.

The old Crump Mill has burned down,It was one of the few old landmarks. Things have changed some,I mean lots,and I doubt if you would even know or recorgnize many things in these parts.

I am enclosing two of our pictures.We had fifteen thousand of these made at one time,and have mailed out most of them.Our Barn Dance has changed station time.We go on the air at,8:30,P.M.Eastern Standard time,and runs until 9:30,P.M.Hope you will be able to get it.

Now a little about myself.I am married,and have a little boy seven years old tomorrow,and a little girl five and a half years old.They are all getting along well.I moved to Charlotte,the 18th of May.Spent a part of last summer and fall in New York City broadcasting,and making Phonograph records.I have been making records for a number of years,and have held the championship on the banjo for the state of North Carolina for nine years.I guess somebody will come along some time and give me a good triming.I guess you know that I got my musical talent from my granfather Squire Jim Hendley.Well I must close this letter,and get busy on some radio programs.I hope you will find time to write me again,Remember me to your family.

Sincerely Yours,

Fisher Hendley

600-Hutcheson Avenue,Charlotte,N.C.

LETTER COURTESY THE JIM MILLS COLLECTION

What an awesome piece of documentation relating to the most famous Gibson banjo in the world. He had absolutely no idea whatsoever as to the history of the RB-Granada serial number 9584-3 that was bought that day by Mr. Hendley, or that it just happened to be the same banjo that Earl Scruggs had owned and played all these years. Had I not called this gentleman on the phone, completely out of the blue that day, looking for information on the (other RB-Granada) that his father had purchased that day; this most important account of RB-Granada 9584-3 might have been lost forever.

This banjo would have sold brand new for $200.00, plus $22.00 for a #522 plush lined case, according to the 1935 Gibson catalog. Dewitt Wheless, and Fisher Hendley had become friends while both were working on radio station WBT, and were also fishing buddies. Fisher Hendley had long been a popular musician, and radio announcer at other stations when he came to Charlotte NC, to work at station WBT, in 1934. This typed and signed,

COURTESY THE JIM MILLS COLLECTION

original letter from Mr. Fisher Hendley's hand, on "Crazy Waters Crystals" letterhead, states that he was the reigning NC state banjo champion, and had been for 9 years running. It also states that WBT printed 15,000 of these promotional photos for them to give away as advertisement. These two

COURTESY THE JIM MILLS COLLECTION

photographic postcards were sent with the letter dated June 1934, and prove that Mr. Hendley already had possession of the banjo by June of 1934, and therefore would have to be the absolute earliest known photos taken of RB-Granada, serial number 9584-3. Undoubtedly the most famous Gibson banjo in history.

The most ironic thing for me concerning the history

of this banjo, starts around 1934 or 35, when a then only 10 or 11 year old Earl Scruggs could have possibly been listening to Fisher Hendley on the radio, playing a banjo that he would have absolutely no idea that he would eventually own and make famous someday. Around 1936 or 37, Fisher Hendley decided to sell this banjo and buy a newer one. It seems Mr. Hendley preferred nice and clean, newer looking instruments, and decided to sell it to "Dewitt Snuffy Jenkins" after it had acquired a little wear. Snuffy was another banjo player whom Mr. Hendley had met while working at WBT in Charlotte. By this time, both men were working at station WIS in Columbia SC. Although it's not recorded, we can only speculate that Snuffy Jenkins didn't pay much more than $100.00 to $150.00 for this banjo, as it was already 2 or 3 years old, and probably showing signs of playing wear. We can come to this conclusion because we know Snuffy sold it to a young Don Reno 3 or 4 years later for only $90.00. Snuffy played and recorded several sides with J. E. Mainer, and also the Hired Hands with this banjo. This rare photo of Snuffy Jenkins from around 1939, features RB-Granada, serial number 9584-3, with a white headguard, and also proves that Snuffy was utilizing this devise even before acquiring the now famous factory headguard equipped RB-4 in 1940 (featured in this book) which he played for the remainder of his life.

COURTESY THE JIM MILLS COLLECTION

FISHER HENDLEY CIRCA 1934.

By the late 1930's Snuffy Jenkins had amassed several followers who were listening closing to him on the radio, and also coming to see him play live, at the many school house, and theater shows he was performing at the time. Although Snuffy was well known as a wonderful stage comedian, these few serious followers were not interested in his comedy. They were trying to learn this highly popular newer three fingered style of banjo playing that seemed to have originated in this small area of North Carolina. One of the first to come around was a skinny kid from Buffalo SC, named Donald Reno. Young Reno had been picking and talking with Snuffy for a few years whenever he got the chance. When Snuffy found an original Flathead Fivestring RB-4, that he liked better, he decided to sell the teenaged Reno this RB-Granada for the whopping sum of $90.00. Don is pictured here not long after this sale, playing this Granada with the Morris Brothers. If you look closely you can see it's still sporting its original gold clamshell tailpiece, and also the white headguard

COURTESY THE JIM MILLS COLLECTION

SNUFFY JENKINS CIRCA 1939.

that Snuffy had installed earlier. Reno would have been approximately 14 to 15 years old in this photo from the early 1940's. The Morris brothers, Wiley and Zeke, were one of the earliest bands to feature the standard instrumentation that would later become known as a full Bluegrass band, with acoustic guitar, bass, mandolin, fiddle, and fivestring banjo played in the 3 finger style. A very young Earl Scruggs would also work in this same band only a few years later.

COURTESY THE JIM MILLS COLLECTION

DON RENO APPROXIMATELY 14 YEARS OLD CIRCA 1941 PLAYING RB-GRANADA S.N. 9584-3 WITH THE MORRIS BROTHERS.

For a little more than two years, from Dec. 1945 until Feb. 1948, Earl Scruggs and Lester Flatt worked together in Bill Monroe's band, as members of The Bluegrass Boy's. This band is considered today the absolute foundation, and cornerstone of the style of music that was later to be called "Bluegrass". Flatt and Scruggs parted company with Monroe in the early part of Feb. 1948, and started their own band, "The Foggy Mountain Boys". Early in 1949 Earl and Don Reno decided to trade banjos. This trade is now legendary. To learn more about this famous trade see "The Don Reno RB-75", featured in this book. In essence Earl traded Don a very clean 1938 RB-75, now known as "Nellie" for this RB-Granada. Reno threw in a Martin guitar as boot, because this Granada was in such rough condition. Not long after acquiring this Granada, Earl had to have several things repaired on it. It seems this banjo had quite a bit of wear and tear from a rough life. Fisher Hendley had played it hard for 3 years, then Snuffy had played it, and traveled with it for approx. 4 years, and then Reno played it pretty hard for 3 more years before entering the military in 1943. While in the Military he left the banjo at home, not realizing that he had left a cake of fiddle rosin inside the case. When he returned home a few years later, he found the rosin had gotten hot and melted inside the case, and all over the Granada. He tried to clean it off, but it took chunks of finish and gold plating off with it. Don then continued to play it hard for 4 more years. So you can imagine the appearance of this RB-Granada banjo when Earl first acquired it, even though it was only 15 years old at the time. Earl told me personally that.. "the banjo looked terrible, and was the color of an old copper penny that had been left laying out in the sun and rain for a few years". That's why Reno threw in the Martin guitar on the trade. There were other serious problems beyond cosmetics concerning the banjo also. The original tensionhoop was cracked,

SLIGHTLY CUT MASTERTONE LABEL LIKE ALL OTHERS KNOWN IN THIS LOT.

NAME AND SERIAL NUMBER IN RESONATOR HAND ENGRAVED BY EARL HIMSELF.

and needed replacing badly. One aspect of being a professional banjo player in those days that most modern banjo players can hardly comprehend today, is how frequently the old calfskin heads may have had to be changed because of breakage in those days, especially if you were a traveling professional musician and playing a lot regularly. I asked Earl how often he changed heads in those years, and he said anywhere from 6 to 7 heads a year. That's a new head nearly every 8 weeks! Another thing to consider is.. these heads were extremely expensive. A new mounted "Joseph Rogers Three Star" calfskin banjo head was priced at $7.50 in late 1930's Gibson catalogs, when a brand new RB-75 was priced at only $75.00!!!. That's exactly 10% of the cost of the whole banjo. At today's prices, on a new $3500.00 banjo, that would be close to $350.00 for one banjo head alone!! These calf skin heads could also prove to be troublesome to mount on a banjo, if conditions weren't good. This could cause warping or breaking of the fragile pre war pot metal tensionhoops if everything didn't sit just exactly right. This explains a lot about the extensive wear and tear on this particular banjo at only 15 years old. This also explains the many broken and replaced tensionhoop's found today on a lot of these old banjos from this same period that were played regularly. The average Calfskin head requires quite a bit more tension, in pounds per square inch of torque, than a modern plastic banjo head to sound their best, and they are also constantly moving around expanding and contracting with the humidity levels. The tension on the newer plastic head, once it has stretched into place, remains pretty much even and consistent throughout their life. They don't expand or contract hardly at all after that.

If you really stop and think about it, this banjo, RB-Granada, serial number 9584-3, has never been owned by an amateur, and just played leisurely at home occasionally. It has been played hard from the day it was shipped out of the factory and delivered, by working traveling musicians for its entire existence. The original gold clamshell tailpiece also appears to have been removed not long after Earl got the banjo. If you look closely at the photo I acquired from Benny Sims from the 1949 Flatt and Scruggs Mercury recording session on page 90, which yielded the original recording of "Foggy Mountain Breakdown", you can see the cheaper budget type of tailpiece fitted to the banjo. This would have been only a matter of months, less than a year after Earl acquired the banjo. All these minor problems aside, Earl must have still heard something down deep inside this banjo. A tone that he knew was something

"THAT MAJESTIC NUMBER 9584-3".

special, and I'll have to say that he surely figured out how to bring it out of it! It has been misprinted many times that Snuffy Jenkins purchased this banjo from a pawnshop for a minor sum of money. This was recently printed in a modern printing of Earl Scruggs book, and I alerted Mr. And Mrs., Scruggs of my research, and findings, but it was too late to change the text in their book. I have researched the history of this banjo extensively, and spoke personally with both families and all facts point to the irrefutable conclusion that Snuffy purchased this banjo from the original owner, Mr. Fisher Hendley. I just wanted to clear that up here also. Snuffy did buy a banjo from a SC pawnshop for $40.00, but it wasn't this banjo, it was the RB-4 Flathead Mastertone, serial number 9639-1, also featured in this book that he would play for the rest of his life. Snuffy told this story so many times publically, and in print, that I'm sure in his later years, even he got confused as to which banjo he was speaking of occasionally. I also think he may have thought that the pawnshop story, although true on the RB-4 banjo, was so good that he used it from time to time on this Granada also, being that it was now famously owned and played by Earl Scruggs. It is a good story, and Snuffy did in fact own both of these great banjos at the same time in 1940, but the truth is.. he did buy the Granada from Mr. Hendley, and the RB-4, he purchased from the Spartanburg SC pawnshop in 1940, for $40.00.

COURTESY THE JIM MILLS COLLECTION

FLATT AND SCRUGGS CIRCA 1957, FEATURING "BOW TIE" INLAY IN THE ORIGINAL RB-GRANADA NECK.

Not long after obtaining it, Earl decided that the original neck on this Granada was too big, and shaped it himself to some degree with a wood rasp, he later decided to send it back to the Gibson factory to reshape the neck, and also for replacement of the broken tensionhoop, and other very worn metal parts. The banjo was also badly in need of a fret job. After what seemed like forever to Earl, the banjo came back with a completely new fingerboard with the then popular "Bow Tie" inlay pattern. This was a common practice of the Gibson factory at this time. You have to remember that these particular banjos didn't have any collector value whatsoever at this time, and saving the original parts, and fingerboard meant absolutely nothing to a busy factory repairman trying to simply turn out another repair job. "Time" was money, and the time required to complete a professional fret job on an older, and more than likely grooved, and worn out fingerboard wasn't worth their effort. The Gibson factory would simply slide a hot knife under the old fingerboard, and slice it off completely, replacing it with a brand new fingerboard of the period featuring the "Bow

COURTESY THE JIM MILLS COLLECTION

FLATT & SCRUGGS" IN AUTHOR'S HOMETOWN OF RALEIGH N.C. ON WPTF RADIO CIRCA 1952. NOTE "BOWTIE INLAY" IN THE FINGERBOARD OF RB-GRANADA SN, 9584-3.

Tie" inlay pattern. As I say, this was a common practice of the factory at the time, and also for many years afterward. I've seen and owned numerous original pre war Gibson banjos from the 20's and 30's missing their original fingerboards because of this procedure. Also the Gibson Company wasn't building any sort of Gold plated banjo at that time, so the only replacement metal parts available were those from the nickel plated banjos they were currently building. Earl decided to have the flange, tensionhoop, armrest, and brackets replaced, as so many of the originals were already broken, worn or in overall bad shape. However, he told me that he instructed the factory not to alter the original plating on the tonering. I think that Earl was very wise to have the foresight and knowledge even at this early time, long before anyone ever spoke of an original flathead tonering, to ask them to not to mess with the original plating on this important part, and left it with its original gold plating intact. He also instructed them not to alter the original finish on the rim. Earl played this banjo with the original Granada neck with this Bow Tie inlay pattern up until approximately 1958 when he had Mike Longworth cut out a Hearts and Flowers pearl inlay pattern, and had Walt Pittman of California build him another neck for this banjo, including a new set of Mr. Pittman's cam type D tuners. Earl has had several necks on this banjo over the years, including a mahogany neck from J. W. Gower of Nashville, and another maple neck from Jim Faulkner of Indiana. All were H&F inlay pattern necks, but Earl is a little uncertain of exact dates as to when these necks were installed and replaced.

In the 1960's there was talk, mainly among musicians, of a few unscrupulous repair people, and also the Gibson factory robbing the original metal parts on these banjos, and replacing them with newer parts. Around this same time Earl just happened to

"EARL SCRUGGS" ENGRAVED IN SCRIPT INTO THE WOOD RIM IN THE UNDENIABLE HAND OF MR. EARL SCRUGGS.

brand his banjo with an electric engraver with identification incase of theft, or tampering. He engraved his name, or initials in several places on his banjo, and they can still be clearly seen today in the detailed photos. Unknowingly again to most, this changing out of old parts for new was not an act of theft by the Gibson company at all, but standard factory procedure, as we spoke of earlier. Again there was no thought of collector value in those days, and it was just standard procedure. Nevertheless, stories began to be spread, and many thought they were being ripped off, and followed Earl's lead in scratching their names, social security numbers, drivers license numbers, and anything else they felt like at the time, with whatever tool they could find I might add, into the rims, resonators, back of pegheads, and all sorts of other places on these old original banjos. I've seen and owned many of these banjos with this act performed on them also. Just take a look at the Mack Crow RB-75's rim featured in this book to see more of this. In 1958 Earl decided that he wanted a new neck made for this banjo, and commissioned Walt Pittman to build him a mahogany neck to be fitted with a fingerboard featuring the original old "Hearts and Flowers" inlay pattern, cut and inlaid by Mr. Mike Longworth. He also wanted a few extra inlays added at the 1st and 15th fret positions. This pattern with the extra inlays was not standard on this particular Granada's original inlay pattern, but Gibson did use this same exact Hearts and Flowers pattern on several style 4 and Granada banjos during the 1930's.

BACK OF RESONATOR SHOWING NEWER FACTORY "GRANADA" SUNBURST FINISH.

On Friday February, 24th of 2006, I spent most of the day with Earl in his beautiful home just outside of Downtown Nashville. I did play a few tunes on this RB-Granada banjo, which I always look forward too, but we didn't pick a whole lot, we mainly just talked about the old days. I feel very fortunate to have gotten to ask Earl about many things I'd always wondered about, but had never really gotten the chance to ask.

A few months previous to this visit, while riding on Ricky Skaggs tour bus somewhere in America, I had a thought just come to me that I'd never heard anyone ask of Earl. We know without a doubt that Earl did send this RB-Granada back to the factory sometime very late Dec. of 1949, or early 1950 as he recorded with it Dec. 11th 1949, and it still had its original Hearts and Flowers inlay and had not yet been sent anywhere. We also know that the banjo was there at the factory for several months after it was sent, while being repaired. I remem-

"E.S." ENGRAVED ON ORIGINAL GOLD PLATED GRANADA TONERING.

bered Earl saying, "he didn't think he would ever get it back", so it just came to me to ponder this... what banjo did Earl play while the Granada was away at the factory at this time? The Flatt and Scruggs show schedule was busier than ever at this time, and they surely didn't slow down one bit just because Earl had sent his banjo off for repair. So after thinking about this to some degree, I had a few questions in my mind to ask of Earl on this sunny February day. I'd hoped to clear up several things, once and for all, and get the story straight from the man himself. First, did he send just the Granada neck back to the factory for repair, or did he send the whole banjo? If he'd kept the Granada pot at home, did he bolt another neck on it, and continue playing it on the road while the original neck was being repaired? Then, if he'd sent the whole RB-Granada banjo back to the factory, how long did they keep it, and what did they replace as far as metal, etc., and then the most interesting question of all for me was..... If he had sent the whole Granada back to the factory, what other banjo did he play for that long period of time while the Granada would remain away at the factory for repair? The Gibson factory was mainly set up to mfg and sell new instruments, and they were notorious for keeping instruments an extraordinarily long time for repair, as repair was more than likely not very profitable for them. Approx. 6 to 9 months wait wasn't unheard of. Another question I had was... what had happened to the original neck from this Granada, a few years later when he abandoned using it for good. Well I'm glad to report that at 82 years young, Earl had a wonderful memory concerning most of these things, and was able to answer nearly all of my questions most definitely. Earl told me that when they moved from WCYB in Bristol VA, in March of 1949 to WROL in Knoxville TN, that he knew he wanted to send the Granada back to the factory for repair, and one of the first things he did was to have Lester advertise live on the air, that Earl Scruggs was looking for a Gibson banjo! Well, shortly thereafter a lady called the radio station, and said her late husband had bought a Gibson Mastertone banjo new back in the 1930's, and had recently passed away, and that she would sell it if Earl was interested in it. When Earl responded to the lady by phone, she told him that she was in the local Knoxville area, and that the banjo was in very good condition, except that one

"E. SCRUGGS" ON ARMREST ENGRAVED BY EARL.

of the tuners didn't work and was broken. When Earl went to see the banjo, the only thing wrong with it was the second string tuner screw had backed out and needed tightening. Earl told me this was a standard 1930's model RB-3 Mastertone, and was really a fine banjo. Isn't that the coolest thing! Wouldn't it be great to be able to find and purchase an original flathead fivestring Mastertone like that today? This is the banjo Earl played while the RB-Granada was sent back to the factory for repair. This photo from the collection of my good friend Jerry Keys, who's a fine banjo player himself, and also a serious Flatt and Scruggs collector, plainly shows Earl playing this standard RB-3 banjo, circa fall of 1949 or early 1950 in Lexington KY while working at the Clay Gentry Arena. The photo is from a local newspaper clipping. Note..this RB-3 had already been sent back to the factory at some point before Earl purchased it, and had its factory Bow-Tie fingerboard installed, but the style 3 peghead inlay is plain as day!

COURTESY THE JERRY KEYS COLLECTION

EARL SCRUGGS PLAYING STANDARD 1930'S RB-3 WHILE RB-GRANADA 9584-3 WAS AWAY AT FACTORY FOR REPAIR. CIRCA 1950.

While at the factory for repair, this RB-Granada had all its metal parts, except the original gold plated coordinator rods, resonator lugs, and its original gold plated, 20 hole Flathead tonering replaced with Gibson's period nickel plated metal, which was all the factory was producing at that time. Although the Gibson Company was not even producing a Mastertone banjo at this early postwar time, they were already featuring the Bow-Tie inlay on their RB- 150 banjos, and they also installed maybe the first postwar style, engraved pearl "Mastertone" block into this fingerboard, as the first Mastertone style 250 banjos didn't come on the scene until 1954 . Earl had let it be known very strongly, not to alter the original gold plated Flathead tonering, or the wood rim in any way. The factory did in fact take a few thousandths off of the diameter of the rim to better fit the newer post war sized flange, but after finish touch up this would have been totally undetectable at the time to Earl. The original fingerboard was removed, and replaced with the then current Bow-Tie inlaid fingerboard. This was something Earl hadn't really ask for except that he'd requested a new fret job, but as said earlier, this was standard factory procedure at the time for repair situations. The neck was also refinished at this time, after being cut down to the size Earl had requested. The factory had warned Earl earlier that the neck may bow or warp if taken down as much as he'd requested, which is exactly what it did a few years later, after it was returned to him. He played this original Granada neck with the Bow-Tie fingerboard for approximately 8 years, even with occasional tuning problems from warping, until 1958, when

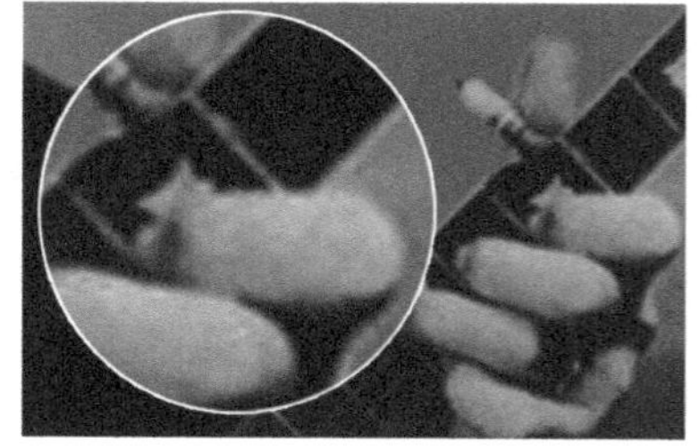

he had the earlier mentioned neck commissioned, and later changed necks again in the 1960's. You can see in these photos from

1956, that Earl was trying different ways to make this original Granada neck note out true. Note the small nail he installed in front of the 4th fret to help the 3rd string intonate more true. The outcome of this most important original five string Granada neck is somewhat uncertain, as both Louise and Earl were still unsure if they'd simply thrown it away and left it in a previous home after moving years ago, or they thought it possibly could have been refurbished and installed into another banjo after adding a newer fingerboard and peghead overlay to hide all its alterations, and then sold by Earl on some "parts banjo" long ago in the late 50's or early 60's. Wouldn't that be something to find out that you owned this neck on some old parts banjo that you'd bought years ago!! It could still be out there somewhere! I don't think most folks actually realize all of the advancements that Earl Scruggs really gave us by experimenting on this one particular instrument. These were ingenious major advancements that have greatly benefitted all of us banjo pickers for the past 50 years or more now. We take it all for granted, and think that it was just always that way. One of the biggest things that as far as I can tell that was totally Earls own idea, and invention, was the addition of 5th string spikes, allowing a player to change keys and still play out of an open G position. This is something Earl and I discussed at length in his home that day in Feb. 2006. Earl told me that before he decided to try out for Bill Monroe in 1945, that he'd had very little time to study Bill's music. He quickly discovered that Monroe wasn't just playing in the standard old open keys of.. G, C, D, like most old time and country musicians of the day were using. He was playing in chords like A, B natural, B flat, and F and other rarely used chords of the period. Earl soon learned that he needed to figure out a way to continue playing the banjo in open G tuning in chords like A, B flat, and B major. He did this by taking hair pins, cutting and bending them and installing them into the fingerboard creating the first known 5th string spikes. Genius! Another invention is the D-tuner. We all know how much that little invention effected bluegrass banjo playing. This one RB-Granada banjo was there in Earl's hands, at that all important moment, when he first got the inspiration, for these many idea's that turned out to be monumental in furthering Bluegrass banjo playing. This banjo has truly been the guinea pig for all these experiments over the years, and has come through it all remarkably well. One thing is for sure, this Granada has always sounded exceptional in Earl's hands. It's almost as if they are spiritually connected. I guess that's what happens when you pick one banjo, nearly exclusively, for 60 years. I would like to thank Earl publically for allowing me to come into his home and photograph this banjo for the world to see. His playing has meant more to me than he will ever know, and more than mere words can say.

EARL SCRUGGS 2008.

Thanks Earl...

PROVENANCE:

1. Shipped from the factory to Jim Graves Barber shop in Wadesboro NC ca. spring 1934

2. Fisher Hendley, by June 1934

3. Dewitt "Snuffy" Jenkins, ca. 1936-37

4. Don Reno, ca. 1940

5. Earl Scruggs, ca. 1949 to Date

The Hoke Jenkins RB-6

SERIAL NUMBER 9434-1

The Hoke Jenkins RB-6

The first knowledge we have of this banjo existing is when Mr. Hoke Jenkins purchased it secondhand, sometime around 1950, from its original owner, who was believed to have been a Doctor in or around Danville Virginia.

Jesse McReynolds of "Jim and Jesse" fame relayed this story to Phillip Jenkins, current owner of the banjo in 2005, he's also Hokes nephew. Hoke was working in a band that included Jim and Jesse at this time, as this fine photo from 1952 attests. Isn't that a great photo! They weren't making any repo necks in 1952!

COURTESY PETE KUYKENDALL

Hoke Jenkins was a nephew of the early pioneer of the North Carolina 3 fingered style, Snuffy Jenkins, and learned the style directly from his uncle Snuffy. Hoke began playing in and around the Carolina's with several bands in the early 1940's, including Carl Story's Rambling Mountaineers.

Hoke recorded some of the earliest Jim and Jesse classic's such as the original cut of "Are You Missing Me", and several others with this featured RB-6 Flathead banjo. This RB- 6 features a very narrow neck in width. There is absolutely no doubt as to the authenticity of this neck being 100% factory original 5 string, but it's extremely narrow width, especially from the 12th fret back to the pot, leads one to believe that it could have possibly been made from what was originally intended to be a plectrum neck blank. Several plectrums were made in the style 6, but so far as we know, this is the only known Original Fivestring Flathead RB- 6 in existence. It's also the only two piece flange banjo featured in this book, and therefore has the fiddle shaped peghead instead of the double cut design. This extremely rare banjo was manufactured by Gibson in the 1930's, and is an original RB fivestring flathead, and therefore deserves its rightful place beside the rest featured in this book, even though it's of the earlier 2 piece flange design. I know of a very few one piece flange style 6 tenors and plectrums, but they are very rare. The finesse involved in engraving the flanges on these models was very difficult to accomplish on the pot metal of the one piece flanges, but the solid brass construction of the 2 piece flange design worked well. They were easier to engrave, and were therefore used more often on the higher grade gold plated, and engraved model's. This is why we see many models higher in grade than the Granada, such as Bella Voce's, Florentine's, and All American's, which all featured engraved flanges, remaining as 2 piece flange models even up into the late 30's when the newer one piece flange had basically been adopted on all other styles. There are a few style 6's and higher grades found with one piece flanges, but again, they are extremely rare indeed.

STYLE 6 BINDING AROUND HEEL AREA.

The style 6 offered two different varieties of binding decoration, the checkerboard pattern as it's known today, and also the gold sparkle. This style 6 banjo features checkerboard binding on its neck, and resonator. Combine the fancy sunburst stained curly maple wood, gold plating, and engraved metal parts, and this creates a very handsome banjo indeed. The engraving pattern on the style 6 seems to have been based on an intricate "X" pattern that's featured on the tonering, flange, and tensionhoop, with hatch marks inside the X's. It also features a beautiful scroll pattern engraved on the armrest. The style 6 was also somewhat of a rarity compared to all the other Gibson banjo models of the time, in that it featured an ebony fingerboard. At this time all other fingerboards were made of either Brazilian rosewood or celluloid, now known as pearloid in the trade. The reason for this substitution is speculated to have been that the very visible black and white, checkerboard binding, that ran over onto the top and sides of the fingerboard, clashed with the red colored rosewood, so the more closely matching black ebony was used instead. The curly maple wood used for the neck and resonators was of a very high grade also, and the finish color listed in the catalog description for the style 6 was "Argentine Grey" which doesn't really make a lot of sense, as it's not very gray in color at all. It's actually a very beautiful amber, golden brown sunburst, very much like that of the

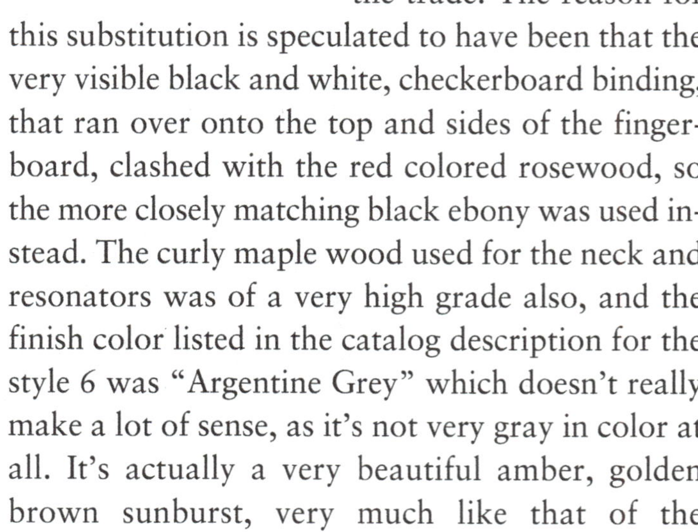

BACK OF PEGHEAD OVERLAY ALL IN ONE PIECE, WITH NO EARS SHOWING, ALSO GROVER TWO BAND TUNERS WITH ORIGINAL SOLID MOTHER OF PEARL BUTTONS.

Granada, but slightly more greenish yellow in hue, and less red. The inlay pattern seems to have been a fancy variation of the old Hearts and Flowers pattern, but more elaborate, with an almost eagle like talon inlay featured in the peghead. These banjos were very elaborate in decoration which was the preference of most every tenor and plectrum player of the day, and their price reflected this at $300.00, upon its introduction in the late 1920's. This was a full $100.00 more than the gold plated, engraved Granada in these depression dollar days. This goes well with the story of it being originally purchased by a Doctor, a man who could have afforded such an extravagance as this, in the then depression stricken South. This banjo features a high profile 20 hole flathead tonering, but since I didn't get to weigh the ring, I don't know if it is of full weight or not. For some odd reason, it seems Gibson experimented with the style 6 more than any other model concerning tonerings. Three distinctly different styles of flathead tonering appear in this same model banjo, along with the 40 hole archtop ring, at approximately the same period of time. The first is the Low Profile flathead ring, as it's known in the flathead banjo world. This ring will interchange perfectly on the rim of an archtop tonering equipped banjo with no modifications. Its profile is quite a bit lower in height on the inner cut, and lighter in weight overall to allow this. The next ring is known as the High Profile, light weight ring. This ring is similar in profile to the full weight ring, but lacks in overall mass, and usually weighs several ounces less than the full cut, full weight rings, which are so desirable for their tone and power. The last and most desirable tonering is the full cut, full weight flathead tonering, known simply as the High Profile, full weight, flathead ring. This type ring is the most desirable of all where sheer power and tone are sought, and is also the model the Gibson Company would adopt as its standard flathead tonering.

STYLE 6 ENGRAVING ON 2 PC FLANGE, TONERING AND TENSIONHOOP.

FIDDLE PEGHEAD DESIGN WITH STANDARD STYLE 6 CHECKERBOARD INLAY PATTERN.

They continued to utilize this type flathead tonering until banjo production ceased during WWII. Every other banjo featured in this book has this type of tonering. The loosely excepted standard on a full weight, High Profile Flathead tonering, if there is such a thing, is approximately anywhere from 2 pounds 14 ounces to approximately 3 pounds 6 ounces. Anything much lighter in weight I think some of the earliest recordings of Bluegrass music. It's 100% original with the exception of a few very minor things, such as one of the screws in the truss rod cover, and the tailpiece screw, which are nothing to hardly even speak of. Another interesting note, which shows the capabilities of the Gibson factory at this time involving banjo rims, is the top layer of wood on this rim. As you can plainly see

UNCUT, BUT BADLY SCRATCHED MASTERTONE LABEL, SHOWING FACTORY SPLICE IN RIM WHERE IT WAS BUILT UP FROM AN ARCHTOP RIM TO CREATE A FLATHEAD BEFORE LEAVING THE FACTORY.

could be considered a high profile light weight ring. Although some of the lighter weight flatheads sound really good, they generally lack a little of the power, and depth that their heavier weight cousins have, and therefore don't command as much respect, or bring the prices of the full weight tonerings. Original Flathead rings much lighter than 2 pounds 12 ounces are rarely encountered anyway.

This RB-6 serial number 9434-1 is an extremely rare banjo, with an important history linking it to from the photographs, a layer of wood was grafted onto the top of this rim at the factory before the original Mastertone guarantee label or finish was applied. This indicates that this banjos rim was originally cut down, and more than likely was intended for an archtop tonering, and the factory simply decided it would instead have a flathead ring installed before shipping out. This type of work was very commonly done by the Gibson factory, as many banjos have been seen completely original with factory altered rims, before they ever left the plant. The Gibson Company was never known for being wasteful, and certainly had the capabilities to complete just about any type of alteration to a banjos rim. The presence of the full uncut, even though badly scratched Mastertone label over this graft, and original unaltered finish leave no doubts as to this banjos 100% originality. Another reason the factory could have possibly made these alterations, was the presence of a defect in the wood not showing up until late in the final lathing of the rim.

COURTESY PHILLIP JENKINS

This RB-6 was owned and played by Hoke Jenkins for several years, until his death, and it descended to his brother Oren, also another fine 3 fingered style player from the Jenkins clan of Harris North Carolina. Oren played this banjo until his death, and it descended to his son Phillip Jenkins, another fine 3 finger style player in the long line of Jenkins Banjo men. I want to thank Phillip again for graciously allowing us to photograph this fine example for this book, and also for the great photos of it. Featured are a few photos of Oren Jenkins playing this banjo in the 1960's from a newspaper article,

COURTESY PHILLIP JENKINS

and also this later photo of Oren sitting around the stump of the huge old oak tree that shaded the Jenkins Family Homeplace for many years, in Harris NC, where... Snuffy, Hoke, Oren, and Phillip Jenkins all learned that 3 finger style!

COURTESY PHILLIP JENKINS

ORIGINAL SMALL GAUGE FRETS, FRICTION 5TH PEG, AND 5TH STRING NUT.

This banjo hasn't been molested at all, and still features its original but very worn frets! The original five stringed tensionhoop is plainly shown, as well as the factory drilled hole in the clamshell tailpiece. These Grover clamshell tailpieces were used on nearly all the higher grade model of Mastertone banjos, and were of a higher grade than their standard budget "Presto" model tailpiece. These double hump clamshell, and also the 4 hump clamshell Grover tailpieces engraved very well, and were used on many models of original pre war Gibson "fivestring" banjos. It's an interesting fact to note that all of these higher grade Grover tailpieces were manufactured with only four fingers, or hooks on the back for the strings. If you think about this fact, it plainly shows just how few "original 5 string banjos" of this caliber or grade, were being manufactured at this time by any company.

ORIGINAL FACTORY DRILLED HOLE FOR THE 3RD STRING IN CLAMSHELL TAILPIECE (NOTE: ALSO SEE MACK CROW RB-75 TAILPIECE FOR SAME FACTORY DRILLED HOLE.

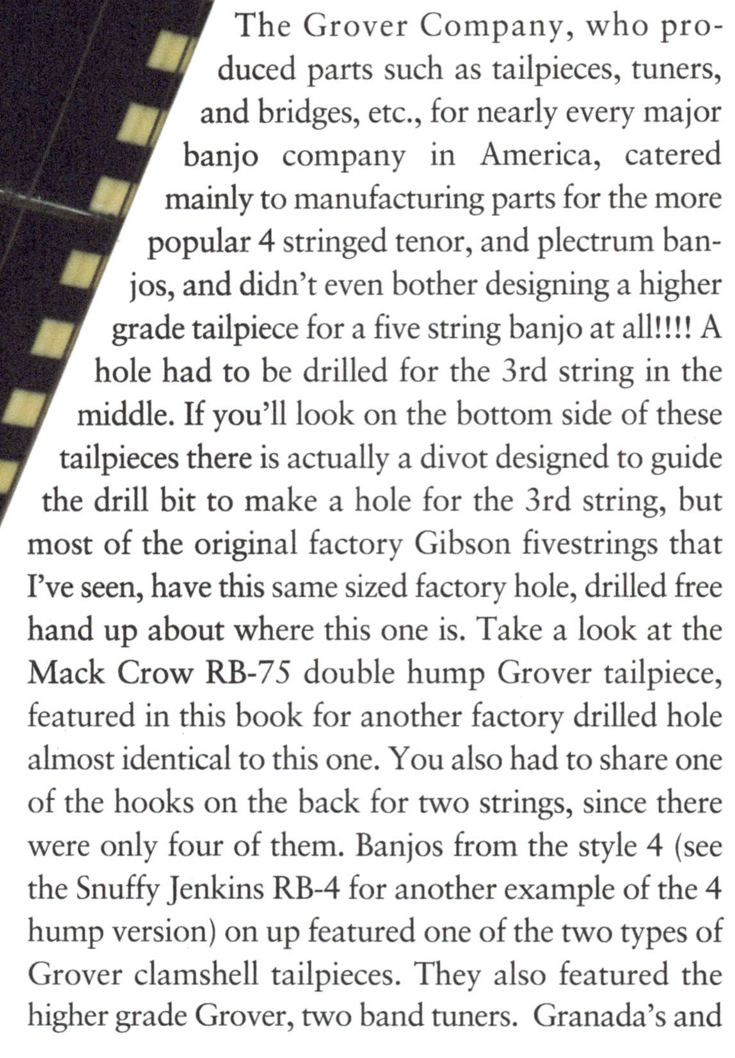

The Grover Company, who produced parts such as tailpieces, tuners, and bridges, etc., for nearly every major banjo company in America, catered mainly to manufacturing parts for the more popular 4 stringed tenor, and plectrum banjos, and didn't even bother designing a higher grade tailpiece for a five string banjo at all!!!! A hole had to be drilled for the 3rd string in the middle. If you'll look on the bottom side of these tailpieces there is actually a divot designed to guide the drill bit to make a hole for the 3rd string, but most of the original factory Gibson fivestrings that I've seen, have this same sized factory hole, drilled free hand up about where this one is. Take a look at the Mack Crow RB-75 double hump Grover tailpiece, featured in this book for another factory drilled hole almost identical to this one. You also had to share one of the hooks on the back for two strings, since there were only four of them. Banjos from the style 4 (see the Snuffy Jenkins RB-4 for another example of the 4 hump version) on up featured one of the two types of Grover clamshell tailpieces. They also featured the higher grade Grover, two band tuners. Granada's and any banjo higher up featured the two band, 4 to 1 ratio, gold Grover tuners with solid mother of pearl tuning buttons, which this banjo still retains, along with its original friction 5th peg, and original nut.

Original five string flathead Mastertones of any model are hard to find, and welcome in almost any condition. But banjos in this wonderful state of preservation rarely turn up. Phillip relayed a beautiful story to me of how much his father Oren loved this banjo. During hard times in the 1960's, Oren Jenkins had the misfortune of his house catching fire in the middle of the night. Phillip said after making sure his family was safe, the only thing his father was able to save was the refrigerator, so they would have food to eat, and this banjo. He ran back into the flaming house, risking his life, to save this banjo. Well I for one, am very glad that this banjo wasn't lost forever, and I'm also very thankful to Phillip, and the whole Jenkins family for their contribution to our music, and also for sharing this wonderful banjo with the rest of us.

PROVENANCE:

1. Purchased new by unknown Doctor around Danville VA circa. 1930's

2. Purchased from him by Hoke Jenkins circa. 1951

3. Descended to Hoke's brother Oren Jenkins

4. Descended to Oren's son Phillip Jenkins

ORIGINAL FACTORY 5 STRING TENSION HOOP AND VERY NARROW NECK HEEL.

SHOWS SERIAL NUMBER AND LABEL TOGETHER ON SAME SIDE, AGAIN THE FACTORY SPLICE IN RIM BUILDING IT UP.

SERIAL NUMBER IN RED PAINT INSIDE RESONATOR, WHICH WAS COMMON AT THIS TIME.

The Bill Worrell
RB-75
SERIAL NUMBER 445-4
Gibson
MASTERTONE

The Bill Worrell RB-75

This banjo shipped from the factory October the 11th, 1937 to Jenkins Music Co., one of the largest Musical Instrument retailers in the country at the time, dealing in all types of instruments. They were located in Kansas City Mo. Shown in the photo is an original Jenkins Music Company catalog from the mid 1930's. For some reason this banjo did not sell quickly enough here, and was shipped within a year to Beckley Music, a music store located in Beckley West Virginia. This I am told was the only Authorized Gibson dealer in the area, and many famous musicians and singers from this region bought their first Gibson Instruments here. Little Jimmy Dickens told me personally that his first Gibson guitar came from this same store. I've also witnessed original Beckley Music Co. paperwork confirming that Charlie Poole did business there. I know of an original Flathead Fivestring, one piece flange, 1930's RB-4, and another Original Fivestring Flathead RB-Granada, from 1930's, that were also purchased new from this same store.

COURTESY THE JIM MILLS COLLECTION

ORIGINAL 1934 LARGE FORMAT, "JENKINS MUSIC COMPANY" CATALOG, FEATURING GIBSON'S WHOLE BANJO LINE.

The original owner of RB-75, serial number 445-4, was a man by the name of Walker. That's all we know about him for sure. Mr. Walker purchased this fine Flathead Mastertone banjo brand new from Beckley Music in or around late 1937 or early 1938. He kept it for approximately 10 years, and sold it in 1947 for the princely sum of $100.00 to a then 16 year old, William (Bill) Mack Worrell, who kept and played it for the next 55 years. Mr. Worrell had a very good paying job working in a sawmill making .75 cents per hour, and when his father found this banjo, and told him about it, he bought it.

Mr. Worrell was kind enough to relay all of this information to me personally, as I bought the banjo directly from him in November of 2002.

This banjo has a very interesting story concerning the earliest known history of recorded Bluegrass Music. It was featured on some of Bluegrass's earliest recordings, by a band called the "Lonesome Pine Fiddlers" in 1952. Ray Goins the banjo player, was one of the first 3

COURTESY THE JIM MILLS COLLECTION

finger style players to follow in the style of Scruggs, and began playing with the "Fiddlers" in or around 1951. The band signed a recording contract with RCA, and was called to record in Nashville for RCA in1952. Ray Goins was playing a simple RB-100 at the time, with no tonering but knew of this fine old Flathead Mastertone way down in the country that was owned by Bill Worrell. He borrowed this banjo, took it to Nashville, and recorded these now classic recordings with it. A few of the titles recorded with this banjo were "My Brown Eyed Darling", "Dirty Dishes Blues", and several others now considered classics. Along about this same time a very young Larry Richardson borrowed this same banjo to record with also, and tried to buy it, but Mr. Worrell didn't want to sell it.

When my dad and I first went to see this rare specimen of a flathead Mastertone, I'd only heard about it from a good friend, and had a vague idea of what to expect it to look like, with its having the extremely rare full Flying Eagle inlay pattern. I honestly thought that my friend could have been mistaken, and that perhaps it was an RB-4 instead of an RB-75, but when I turned the corner of Mr. Worrell's living room, and saw that thing laying there in the floor, in its original redline case, with the original factory headguard still attached, and all that full Flying Eagle inlay shining up at me, on beautiful dark red stained mahogany wood, my heart absolutely skipped a beat! I remember very well the pounding in my head the whole time Mr. Worrell and I were negotiating the sale of this banjo. I thought it was going to explode! Right after purchasing this banjo, I knew well that its full "Flying Eagle" inlay pattern, as it's known, was very rare to find on a style 75 or 3, and I only knew of two more like it. One of these rare banjos was owned by a hero of mine, Mr. Sonny Osborne, so I called him immediately. Sonny's "Flying Eagle" inlaid RB-75 is the banjo that he recorded "Rocky Top" with, and also many other famous Osborne Brothers hits. When I called Sonny, I simply asked him, how many of these particular banjos did he know of with this rare full Flying

ORIGINAL RB-75 WITH FULL "FLYING EAGLE" INLAY PATTERN OF WHICH ONLY 3 ARE KNOWN TO EXIST.

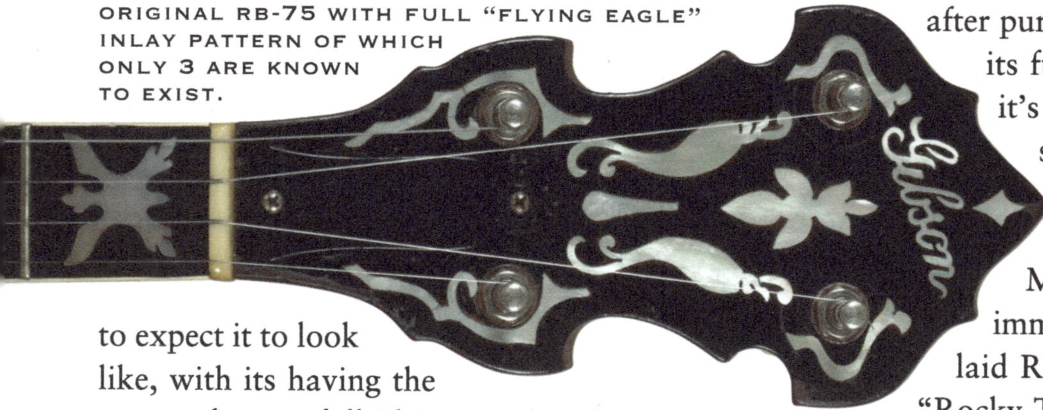

Eagle inlay pattern. He said two for sure and maybe three! Counting his banjo he knew of one other for sure. I asked him where the other one was, he said he'd only seen it once, and played it when he was around 11 or 12 years old, in Camp Creek West Virginia. I was elated to hear this and told him..I've just bought that banjo! This was the same exact banjo, as Sonny had seen and played this banjo while it was on loan to Ray Goins of the Lonesome Pine Fiddlers from Bill Worrell! Sonny's legendary older brother Bobby Osborne had been playing with "The Lonesome Pine Fiddlers" also, and Sonny was visiting with them some during the summer months. I remember Sonny saying that he could remember it like it was yesterday, and could take me to the very house and room where he played it, if it still existed! That was over 50 years ago! Now that's a fine memory. Sonny's Birthday is Oct. 29th 1937, so he and this banjo were born within a few days of each other, and I thought it was very cool that he was the first guy I showed it too after purchasing it.

COURTESY THE JIM MILLS COLLECTION

Mr. Worrell also managed to have hung on to several old black and white photos of this banjo from the time he bought it in 1947, up into the 1950's, which are extremely rare to find today. The featured photo on page 70 is of Mr. Worrell's little brother Gilbert, right after he purchased the banjo in 1947. He said he wanted a photo of it so bad, that he sat his little brother down in this old ladder backed chair, and told him to hold the banjo still. Looking closely into the background of this photo, it's easy to see some of the simple charms of everyday life that existed on the farm. This was Mr. Worrell's childhood West Virginian mountain home in 1947. You can plainly see the mountain's peak in the back, a wire fence from their Hog lot, a corn crib, and half of an old hound dog's tail that was casually walking through when the photograph was taken! Now that's country!

The next photo is from 1947 and features a 16 year old Mr. Worrell playing this banjo in a band called the "Lonesome Valley Boy's". It also features a 14 year old Joe Meadows playing fiddle, who would soon go on to make a name for himself as the Stanley Brothers fiddle player in just a few years. This photo also features a funny little incident to me, when looking closely at the banjos head you will notice a small white square attached just above the bridge. I enquired about this, and Mr. Worrell told me it was a piece of white tape he'd placed there, because the calfskin head had busted! This photo is interesting to me in another way. Besides the presence of the electric guitar, this bands choice of instrumentation would seem normal in any of the many Bluegrass Band's that would pop up throughout the 1950's, a few years after Bill Monroe and his Bluegrass Boy's featuring Earl Scruggs had hit the scene, but the fact of the matter is, this photo was taken in 1947! Earl and Lester were still working in Mr. Monroe's band! It seems that this Bluegrass Music was already taking hold, and being emulated to a certain degree even at this early time. Mr. Joe Meadows and Mr. Worrell were lifelong friends all the way from childhood, and here's another photo of them both picking in the living room from 1952, while Mr. Worrell was home on leave from the Navy. I wonder what 78 record that is on the turntable? I'll bet it's a Flatt and Scruggs record!

COURTESY THE JIM MILLS COLLECTION

Mr. Worrell told me that after moving from WVA to the Salem/Roanoke area of Virginia, that he went to several of the newly popular Bluegrass festivals that had originated there in the mid 1960's. He said that, at some point, nearly every professional banjo player had come up to him, asking to see this banjo, and then had tried to buy it, but Mr. Worrell wasn't quite ready to part with it yet. Mr. Worrell continued to play this old banjo through the 70's, and even built a newer "parts banjo" for himself, and semi retired this old banjo in the 1980's, although he still played it occasionally.

When I learned of this banjo's existence I was thrilled, as I'd been within 10 miles of it hundreds of times in the past 20 years going up and down Interstate I-81, and had never even known that it existed.

This banjo is standard catalog style 75 all the way, with the exception of its rare "Full Flying Eagle" inlay pattern. This is one of the earliest incarnations of the style 75, which was introduced in 1937, previously being designated the style 3, and these early style 75's have features of both earlier style 3's and the new style 75's, such as.. This banjo came with flathead screws in its L brackets, and phillips screws in its trussrod cover. In just a few years they would change almost exclusively to phillips head screws in both. This banjos serial number is still located inside the rim. This is another feature that would change sometime around 1938, when the Gibson Company began stamping the serial numbers into the back of the peghead. This banjo is also stained a darker shade of reddish brown that typifies the style 75's from the earlier style 3's they had replaced a few years earlier. Most of the earlier style 3's had been stained quite a bit lighter than these later produced style 3/75 banjos.

RB-75 serial number 445-4 features a high profile, full weight, 20 hole, Flathead tonering, nickel plating, mahogany neck and resonator, and full uncut Mastertone label inside. It came complete with its original red-line case, headguard, key, instructional papers from the factory, old Gibson string box, and wrench, and many old black and white photos.

In 2005, I was very fortunate to get to record a sort of Pre War Gibson Banjo Documentary CD for Sugar Hill Records titled "Hide Head Blues" featuring four of my Original Flathead Fivestring Mastertone banjos, and this particular banjo was really a stand out for me to play in the studio. I cut two songs with it, and was extremely satisfied with the outcome.

I would like to thank Mr. Worrell for allowing me to purchase such a fine banjo, and I hope that I can enjoy it for half as many years as he did.

FLATHEAD SCREWS WERE STILL BEING USED IN L BRACKETS DURING THIS TRANSITION FROM STYLE 3 TO THE STYLE 75, AND THIS BANJO HAS ITS ORIGINAL PHILLIPS SCREWS IN ITS TRUSSROD COVER.

PERFECT UNCUT MASTERTONE LABEL.

P. S. I forgot to mention that not long after obtaining this banjo, I showed it to Mr. Earl Scruggs in 2002. He remembered very well seeing Ray Goins playing this very banjo at a show featuring "Flatt and Scruggs" and "The Lonesome Pine Fiddlers" in Bramwell WVA around 1952.

There I am, "cold tracking" these old banjos again!

Provenance:

1. Shipped from Kalamazoo MI factory Oct.11th 1937 to Jenkins Music Company in Kansas City MO
2. Shipped from there to Beckley Music Co. in Beckley WVA sometime around late 1937 early 1938.
3. Purchased brand new from Beckley Music Co. by Mr. Walker (late 1937- or early 1938)
4. Purchased by Bill Worrell from Mr. Walker in 1947 for $100.00
5. Purchased by author from Bill Worrell, Nov. 2002

COURTESY THE JIM MILLS COLLECTION

THE AUTHOR AND EARL SCRUGGS HOLDING RB-75 SERIAL NUMBER 445-4, IN EARL'S DRESSING ROOM DURING THE TAPING OF "THE THREE PICKERS" LIVE CD/DVD IN WINSTON SALEM NC, DEC. 2002.

SERIAL NUMBER IS STILL STAMPED INSIDE RIM, BUT NO "PAT APPLIED FOR" STAMPING IS USED AFTER THIS TIME.

SERIAL NUMBERS ALL IN CHALK IN RESONATOR, AS NO RED PAINT WAS USED AFTER THIS TIME.

ORIGINAL 5 STRING TENSION HOOP, AND LARGER STYLE LETTERING IN PEARL MASTERTONE BLOCK.

The Mack Crow
Gold Plated RB-75

SERIAL NUMBER F453-2

The Mack Crow Gold Plated RB-75

This banjo means more to me than most, as I've owned and played it for several years now. I've been blessed and very fortunate to have owned 9 of these wonderful Original Fivestring Flathead Mastertone Banjos, but this one is still my personal favorite. This banjo according to the Crow family was ordered by Mr. Mack Crow sometime around 1939 or 40 as simply a "Gold Plated Mastertone", that's all he asked for. When he received the banjo that they had sent him from the factory, it was their new top of the line, Top Tension model RB-18, for this was the only "Gold Plated Mastertone" model being produced at this time. The Granada, Style 5 Deluxe, Style 6, Bella Voce, Florentine, and All American had all been discontinued by late 1937. Unhappy with the extra weight and mass associated with the Top Tension models, he sent it back to them and asked for a plain old normal "Gold Plated Mastertone"!

COURTESY THE JIM MILLS COLLECTION

COURTESY THE JIM MILLS COLLECTION

The only standard pot construction, non Top Tension Mastertone model being produced at this time was the budget model RB-75, which came standard with a rather plain mahogany neck and resonator, and simple nickel plating, without engraving of any kind. The Gibson factory, never known to disappoint a customer or endorser would build to suit, and they did. On June 21st 1940, they shipped this one of a kind "Gold Plated Mastertone", RB-75, serial number F453-2, along with another standard RB-75 in this same batch, to Valero Music Company.

Mack Crow had been a Gibson endorser dating back to the 1920's, and worked in several different bands in North Carolina, such as the Blue Ridge Ramblers, featured in this early photo from the late 1920's. It's plain to see in the photo that most all of the musicians were playing Gibson instruments from the 1920's. Mack is seen here with the 1920's RB-3, archtop banjo that he played for many years.

Mack Crow was considered one of the very earliest pioneers of the 3 fingered style developed in NC, and was later billed as "The Banjo King of the Carolina's". Late in his life he was featured mainly as a one man show, and did tricks with the banjo such as twirling it, and was considered a really fine entertainer from what I understand. He is mentioned as an early influence by Earl Scruggs in his landmark book "Earl Scruggs and the Five String Banjo".

RB-75 serial number F453-2, **is the Only Factory Original Gold Plated RB-75 known to exist,** and has many custom features. As stated earlier, the previous gold plated engraved models such as the Granada, Style 5 and 6, Bella Voce, and higher models had all been discontinued by 1937, but Gibson never known for being wasteful, still had remaining original gold plated engraved parts from these previously discontinued models still lying around. These surplus parts couldn't be utilized on any of their standard catalogued models, so they were drafted into use to complete this one of a kind "Gold Plated Mastertone" for Mr. Crow. In the late 1930's and early 1940's it was not uncommon to find both gold and chrome plated parts mixed in on a standard nickel plated banjo from this time period. For example take a look at the Curtis McPeake RB-75, known as "Ole Betsy" featured in this book to see a late example of an RB-75 with these features. It has a chrome tonering and a gold plated tailpiece hanger that came originally from the factory that way. Also the "Posie Roach" RB-75, featured in this book came with a chrome tonering originally. So you can see this was not an uncommon practice that the factory hadn't already done on occasion when parts were needed.

ORIGINAL "BELLA VOCE" ENGRAVED TAILPIECE AND "GRANADA" ENGRAVED ARMREST.

This RB-75 serial number F453-2 features a Granada engraved one piece armrest, a Bella Voce engraved, double hump tailpiece, with a factory drilled hole for the 3rd string, and a high profile, Style 6 engraved, full three pound, 3 ounce, original 20 hole Flathead Tonering. The original tension-hoop is gold plated without engraving, as is the original flange. The plating on the flange is worn and seems to have a good amount of the original copper flashing showing through, as someone tried to clean it at some point, and the copper is noticeable mainly on the flange. My friend and fellow banjo scholar Steve Huber and I have had many discussions on gold plating from this period, and have both come to the conclusion that the Copper content, concerning flashing, varied in all the pre war gold plated banjos. It seems that this was a factor left strictly up to whoever was in charge of the flashing that day, before the gold plating process, and some banjos seem to have little to none, while some like this one have a good amount. We've seen several 100% original examples with almost no flashing at

ORIGINAL FACTORY DRILLED HOLE FOR THE 3RD STRING IN TAILPIECE.

all applied with pure old gray pot metal showing underneath, and then some with almost pure copper underneath like this Mack Crow example. After a pre war banjo's gold plating has had time to patina and turn a warmer shade over the years, it seems to create a richer darker hue to the color of the gold plating when more copper flashing was used. This is usually evident in the warmer colored tonerings and flanges seen, as opposed to the brighter and really shiny yellow gold. I believe that the Scruggs Granada's tonering also has a good amount of copper flashing, as it's the same warmer gold color as this Mack Crow banjo. Compare the Sonny Osborne Granada with the Scruggs Granada's color of the tonering and you'll see the difference. I would bet that Sonny's banjo doesn't have quite as much copper content and flashing in its tonering even though they are serial numbered mates. This more shiny looking gold on the tonering is also seen on the Hoke Jenkins RB-6, featured in this book.

The plating on all these banjos mentioned are 100% factory original but do show the variances in copper content and how it affects the gold color. RB-75, Sn F453-2, also came with original gold plated Grover pancake tuners. The funny thing is, the factory left the standard nickel plated coordinator rods, washers, screws, and resonator lugs alone, as if they figured these parts wouldn't be seen anyway from the outside, and they're not.

SERIAL NUMBER STAMPED ONTO THE BACK OF PEGHEAD WITH VERY FAINT "F" STAMP.

Mr. Crow kept this banjo for 12 years, until 1952, when advancing in age, he decided to sell it. He put it up for sale at the highest price ever known to be asked around that part of the country for a banjo.... $500.00. I've spoken with several older gentlemen still living in the area about the banjo, and they were quite entertaining. One older gentleman related the following to me, "Yea I remember it well, hell everybody in that whole damn country down there wanted that banjo, but nobody could come up with the $500.00". This was an extraordinary price at this time for any banjo. Another older gentleman relayed to me, "Yea I remember, it seems like he had it for sale for a good long while, that is until Ole Aiken came up from Statesville and bought it". It seems Mr. Aiken had a good job, and decided that he could afford this banjo, and bought it. Mr. Avery Aiken, a fine local player from the Statesville NC area, had his own band and was well known locally. He kept and played this banjo until his death some 50 years later. I was fortunate enough to have been able to purchase it directly from his widow Mrs. Aiken a few years afterward. This banjo had been played very hard its entire life, and clearly shows the signs of it. I remember seeing this banjo for the first time like it was yesterday. When Mrs. Aiken brought it into the room, I slowly pulled it out of the case and immediately noticed that it had a thick coating of waxy green mold all over the fingerboard and what were left of its frets. The old frets were so worn they were literally worn down into the fingerboard which was also grooved out very badly. The banjo had been under the bed for a good while, and I remember wrapping my hand around that neck and thinking to myself... "Man, this is absolutely the best neck I've ever laid my hands on"! The strings rattled terribly, and the fifth string nut was a wood screw, with the threads sticking through the side of the neck! Even in this totally unplayable state, it was still a very impressive banjo.

It seems that this particular banjo's unique neck shape has singlehandedly sparked an interest in a different neck contour for current neck builders. RB-75 Sn F453-2 has a slight "V" taper in the contour of its neck that is not all that common. I've seen it featured on a few tenors from this late period, but not on many 5 strings. It is extremely comfortable to play, and gives the illusion of being thinner and maybe slightly faster than most necks, but the actual width of the fingerboard is standard size for these banjos, and creates no problems playing at all. If anything it helps. There have been many new banjo builders in recent years to come out with a so called "V" shaped or "Speed Neck" on their banjos, a term that I honestly never heard until this Gold RB-75 surfaced. Some of these new "V" necks that I've seen built by different makers are tapered so sharp that you might think they would cut your hand, but in reality this original RB-75 neck has a very subtle taper, not sharp or overly noticeable at all to the eye or hand. The common definition of speed neck today just means it doesn't have any finish on the back side of the neck. This is again is something I never thought that much about, but when Steve Huber built a replica of this banjo for me, I asked to not have any finish on the back of the neck, as I was used to the original neck which had its finish worn away many years ago. In 2004 Steve Huber and I decided to try and replicate this banjo as close to the original specs as possible, in a signature "Jim Mills Model" Huber banjo that would also include this rare neck shape. I left the banjo in Steve's vault for a few weeks for him to totally spec out from one end to the other, and the results have been wonderful. These banjos are without a doubt the closest thing to the real thing I've encountered in every way, and I continue to play the new "Jim Mills Model" Huber banjo, in most of Ricky Skaggs and Kentucky Thunders live shows. I won't lie and tell you that this new banjo sounds every bit as good as the original, but I will say it's the best sounding new banjo that I've played. When comparing the two banjos as far as "shape and feel", it's so close to the original that if blind folded, I would have a hard time distinguishing one from the other.

STANDARD STYLE 75 INLAY, WITH LARGER LATE STYLE BELL SHAPED TRUSSROD COVER WITH PHILLIPS SCREWS,

The wonderful old original factory gold plating on this RB-75 has long been well worn, and it now reveals hues of copper, brass, and the original gold plating all combined in a warm brown patina.

I once thought of trying to clean it up many years ago, and after scrubbing a small area, I decided that it would look absolutely awful, like a spotted dog, with little spots of gold plating, brass and copper showing through when I was finished, so I left it too patina over nicely, which it has done in a wonderful rich golden brown

AVERY AIKEN'S NAME ENGRAVED ONTO BOTTOM OF ORIGINAL GOLD PLATED FLANGE.

REMNANTS OF 3 SMALL "CROWS FEET" BELIEVED TO HAVE BEEN ENGRAVED INTO PEARL INLAY BY MR. MACK CROW.

color. The back of the neck has little if any finish remaining, but the resonator has survived in a wonderful state, with nearly all its original finish intact. Mr. Aiken must have really played this banjo hard for many years, for when I purchased it, its original neck was in such poor condition that it showed little sign of ever having had any maintenance done to it at all in 50 years. It was absolutely, and completely unplayable. The frets were actually worn down so far that they were imbedded into the wood of the fretboard! The grooves in the fingerboard were so deeply entrenched that they literally looked like corn rows in a field! It still retained its original friction fifth peg, and its original gold pancake tuners had been replaced with 1950's Bow Tie tuners, as the filled holes seen in the back of the peghead attest too. The original gold Grover pancakes were still in the case pocket though, and after a good cleaning, they worked fine, so I had them reinstalled. As soon as I purchased this banjo I sent it straight to Mr. Frank Neat for a fingerboard dressing, and a new fret job. Luckily since the original fingerboard had never been dressed down before, there was still enough thickness left in it for a good board dressing to straighten everything out fine. One thing we discovered while doing this work was a little artwork that we believe Mack Crow may have applied many years before, in the 5th fret inlay, he'd scratched out an engraving of 3 little "Crow's feet" in this pearl inlay, and it was so dirty it hadn't been noticed until Frank got hold of it. You can still see the remnants of this in the photos.

COURTESY THE JIM MILLS COLLECTION

The very next week after its refurbishing I played it on stage with both Dolly Parton and Ricky Skaggs at Merlefest, and it seemed to snap back to life almost immediately, and I noticed it really cut a microphone great. Right away I knew this banjo was something special. It just seemed to have the most unusual ability to nearly play itself. It is so responsive to almost any touch, hard or soft, and will not let you down under any pressure you can give it. I can't describe it too you with words, and I can't write it down on paper, but this banjo gives me a little grace when I need it most. Maybe sometimes when I just don't feel great, and may need a little help to make it through a show. I'll say this banjo makes up for a lot of my shortcomings, and again, it's my favorite banjo for sure. I'm thankful to the Good Lord for it, and pray He'll allow me to keep and play it for a long time. My good friend and banjo scholar Snuffy Smith of King, North Carolina noted the first time he ever heard this banjo that.. "That banjos going to be famous someday" and he has refretted it several times now. Snuffy keeps it in playing shape for me, and I'll say he does a fine job working on all these delicate old original banjos.

This banjo also features a few battle scars from being played so hard and put up wet for over 50 years. It has an old heel crack repair from many years ago, and when I asked Frank Neat about this he said it seemed as strong as could be. It's never given me a problem in all the years I've traveled with it by car, plane, train and bus, so I guess he was right. There are also several identifying features that were added to this banjo after Mr. Aiken acquired it in 1952. Earl Scruggs was as far as I know the first in Bluegrass to scratch his name or initials into his banjo, but it seems that "after Earl did it" it was the "cool thing to do", and most of his faithful fans followed suit, as I've owned many pre war Gibson banjos with names and initials carved into them, but this Gold RB-75 "takes the cake". Mr. Aiken made sure that absolutely nothing would ever be removed from this banjo without his name, initials, Social Security number, or NC Drivers License number being present on it somewhere! As can be seen in the photos he engraved them everywhere.. under the flange, on the side of the tonering in several

"AVERY AIKEN" PERSONALLY CARVED BY MR. AIKEN INTO THE RESONATOR WALL.

BADLY SCRATCHED BUT UNCUT MASTERTONE LABEL, AND 2ND OWNER AVERY AIKEN'S NAME, SOCIAL, AND NC DRIVERS LICENSE NUMBER INSCRIBED INTO RIM.

STYLE 6 ENGRAVING ON TONERING, WHERE ONCE AGAIN MR. AIKEN'S NAME AND NUMBERS ARE ENGRAVED ON THIS ONE OF A KIND, ONLY KNOWN FACTORY ORIGINAL GOLD PLATED RB-75.

places, and also inside the rim beside the Mastertone label. We also have to take into account that (this "was" his banjo and he could do absolutely anything he pleased with it), and also at this time in the world, these banjos were in no way as valuable monetarily as they are today.

Another trait some of these later RB-75's seem to feature is the darker reddish brown color that this banjo displays. This banjo was no doubt played in countless smoky bars and many other rough places throughout its long history, and both the binding and tuner buttons have turned a very rich warm dark golden color that is quite nice looking in contrast with the darker wood color. What do you know? Nicotine "is" good for something!

Several very fine banjo players and scholars alike have noted that this "One of a kind Gold Plated RB-75 banjo" has the most desirable trait of having the best of both worlds as far as Pre War Gibson banjo tone is concerned because it features Mahogany wood in its neck and resonator like a style 75, and then a heavy weight factory Gold plated Flathead tonering the same as a period Granada. It has been my finding that resonator wood type is of little importance concerning banjo tone, as it's mostly made up of a very thin outer ply of whatever type veneer went on that particular model, be it mahogany, maple, or walnut, and all pre war Gibson resonators of the same period (not including the solid wood toptension models) were basically made in the same manner. For instance if you replace a mahogany resonator on a typical 1930's style 3 with a typical plain old rock maple style 1 resonator there isn't $10.00 worth of difference in the actual sound of this same banjo, that is as long as it's being replaced with an authentic period Pre War Gibson resonator. It has also been my finding that neck wood does greatly influence the sound of that same banjo, with mahogany, maple, or walnut being the three most used wood types. In the 1950's Earl Scruggs had a Mahogany neck installed on his Granada banjo, and continued to use this combination of Mahogany neck and gold plated tonering for many years on his Granada. This setup in Earl's hands produced some of the very best recordings of banjo tone known to exist with this completely non standard Gibson produced banjo combination. Gibson, to my knowledge never produced a catalog standard factory mahogany and gold plated banjo. The Factory Gold plated banjos always went hand in hand with either maple or walnut wood. Maple on Granada's, style 6's, and many other higher grades, and also walnut on style 5's, but on the lower priced mahogany banjos, nickel plating was always the standard. I know of a few rare 1920's Granada's that left the factory with style 4 mahogany wood, but they are not typical and are also totally non catalog standard. As far as I know Gibson never made a standard Gold plated, mahogany production line banjo.

Several older gentlemen who knew Mr. Aiken told me that Earl Scruggs had tried to purchase this banjo from Mr. Aiken sometime around 1954 at a local Flatt and Scruggs show, not long after he'd acquired it, but Mr. Aiken didn't want to sell it. I asked Earl about this, and showed it to him years ago, not long after I got it, and he remembered it well. When I pulled it out of the case, he said.. "That banjo came out of Statesville North Carolina"! I'll say he's still got a heck of a memory of good banjos from over 50 years ago!

Here's a photo of Earl absolutely wearing out "Cumberland Gap" on this very banjo in his living room in Nashville TN. When I first saw this photo, I noticed that his fingers were placed exactly where my own fingers had worn the frosting off the head, and I wouldn't take anything for this photo!

This old banjo has served me well, and I've been fortunate enough to get to play it all over the world, and record several good records with it. I don't travel with it as much as I used too, because of the rising values and also the way we travel is not the most consistent thing in the world. On a 4 day road trip we may start off in a tour bus and end up on a plane, and have to get from place to place in a limo or van or who knows what before returning home, and the swapping vehicles has become just too dangerous and too big of a liability for me to worry about and still do my job well. I used to throw it under buses and on airplanes, and played it every week, but unfortunately that's not a very smart thing to do anymore. I miss it, but I still play it on the road as often as I can, when I have more control of my travel arrangements. I also record almost exclusively with it still.

In 2005, I recorded a kind of Pre War Flathead banjo documentary CD for Sugar Hill Records called "Hide Head Blues" that featured 4 of my different Original Flathead Fivestrings, and I still ended up playing this banjo the most!

COURTESY THE JIM MILLS COLLECTION

God Bless Mack Crow, and Avery Aiken for looking after this old banjo for all those years, and I pray that I can "look after it" for a little while longer. I know it's brought a lot of joy to me during my life, and I hope it will continue to bring joy to its next owner. Hopefully long after I'm gone…

PROVENANCE:

1 Shipped from the factory June 21st 1940 to Valero Music Co. for endorser Mr. Mack Crow.

2. Purchased by Avery Aiken in 1952 for $500.00!

3. In possession of author 1997

4. Purchased by author 2001

ORIGINAL BRASS 5 STRING TENSIONHOOP, AND PEARL MASTERTONE BLOCK SHOWING LATE LARGER TYPE LETTERING.

"Nellie"
The Don Reno RB-75
SERIAL NUMBER 518-1

"Nellie" The Don Reno RB-75

The first documented history we have of this banjo is absolute. We are very fortunate to have this high resolution scan of the original shipping ledger showing that RB-75 serial number 518-1, shipped out of the factory March 9th 1938 from Kalamazoo MI., and was delivered to Henry County Furniture Company. Yes I did say RB-75! This banjo has had the misfortune of being wrongly identified in print many times by several people over the years as a 1934 RB-3, and also as an RB-4. This designation of style 75 does not come from my personal observation, nor anyone else's opinion, but is an absolute fact! This original shipping ledger plainly shows when and where it was shipped, and also that it went out with its catalog # 521, redline case, which would have been flannel lined. This furniture store was located in Martinsville Virginia, and evidently sold many Gibson instruments throughout the 1930's and 40's. Check out the Posie Roach RB-75 also featured in this book, as it shipped to this same store less than 26 months later. At this time in America it was quite common for furniture stores, barbershops, jewelry stores, and many other types of businesses to obtain a Gibson dealership, to sell musical instruments, as there were very few true music stores in the rural south. The Gibson Company was trying to expand its territories, and would grant a dealership to most any kind of legitimate business at this time.

The vintage "Church fan" featured in the photo is

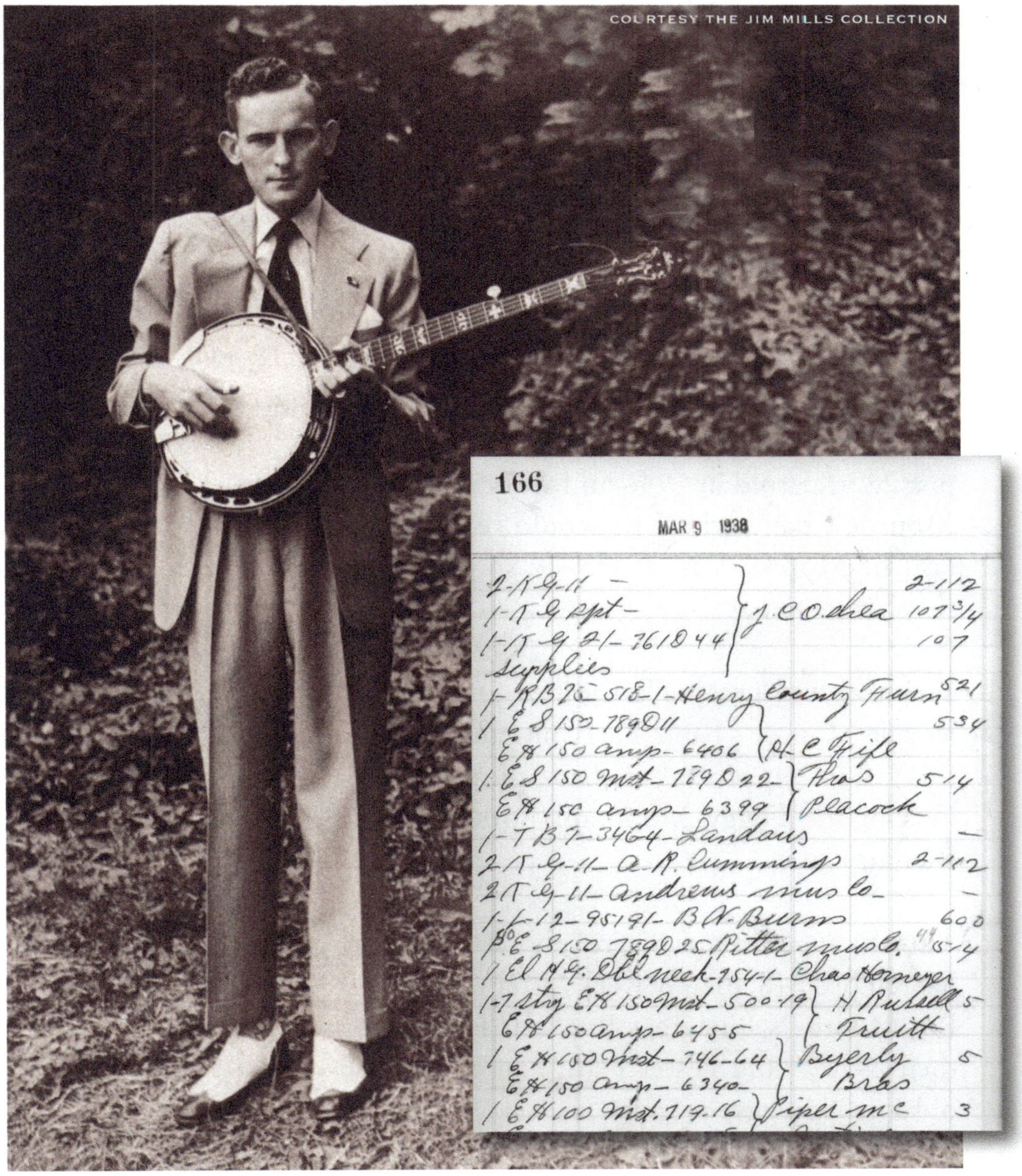

COURTESY THE JIM MILLS COLLECTION

DON RENO WITH NELLIE CIRCA 1949-50 AND THE ORIGINAL SHIPPING LEDGER FOR THIS RB-75.

the only documented proof of the Henry County Furniture Co. ever existing, that I have been able to locate.

COURTESY THE JIM MILLS COLLECTION

The next time this banjo would show up in history was approximately 8 years later, when Earl Scruggs purchased it from its original owner, Mr. Haze Hall from Bassett VA, around the middle of 1946, according to this newspaper article from 1974, which quotes Mr. Hall on this special banjo sale. Earl was just 22 years old in 1946 and working in Bill Monroe's band where he would record several of Monroe's most classic songs using this banjo.

When he and Lester Flatt joined forces after leaving Monroe's band, Earl continued to play this RB-75 on several of the earliest recordings of the Foggy Mountain Boys, for the Mercury label.

This is an extremely rare photo taken in March of 1948, merely weeks after they'd left Bill Monroe's Bluegrass Boy's. It features a then 34 year old Lester Flatt, and a 24 year old Earl Scruggs, at radio station WDVA in Danville VA, where they would first try their hand at making it on their own. This photo is very special to me, as I see two young men, filled with ambition and dreams, but also still unsure of just what may come their way in life, as a newly formed band, seeking to gain their own identity. Earl just recently told me that they were only in Danville less than 2 weeks, and never really got started there because they didn't even have a band organized yet. They'd come to Danville hoping to organize a group, but things just didn't pan out there. Within a few days of this photo they had moved to radio station WHKY in Hickory NC.

E Brides Engagements Books

MARTINSVILLE BULLETIN

ACCENT on PEOPLE

Sunday, June 30, 1974—Page 1-E

Haze Hall and Banjo Are Old Friends

By GINNY RICHARDS
Bulletin Accent Editor

When Haze Hall breaks out his banjo it is a reunion of two old friends.

He swings the instrument out of its golden cloth-lined case with a sweeping motion that might cause tremors among less-experieenced banjo pickers. With Hall, there is little doubt that he knows what he's doing.

Hall roams from country to blue grass music, though he says blue grass is a bit too fast for him now.

"There ain't too much difference between country and blue grass now," he quips as his fingers fly. "They've just changed the name and speeded it up."

Familiar foot-tapping songs swell from the instrument: "Wildwood Flower," theme from the "Beverly Hillbillies," "East Virginia" and "It's Only a Shanty in Old Shantytown."

"That was supposed to be 'The Grandfather's Clock' but it 'bout run down a bit," Hall laughs as he plucks the tune without missing a chord.

Hall says his favorite artists include Bobby Thompson, Roy Clark, Don Reno, Nick Jordan and Earl Scruggs.

"All banjo players have their own style, but now everyone wants to imitate Scruggs," he says.

With some coaxing, Hall reminisces on the Mastertone Banjo he sold Scruggs for $150 in 1946.

"If I had it back now I'd make $1,500," he jokes with a bit of trith.

banjo just took me along."

Hall used to sing and play the mouth harp when he played at area dances and festivals and for radio and television programs, but he doesn't do much of that anymore.

"In the last few years I've gotten away from that," he says. "When you're young you just like to be out someplace. Now I'm happy here at home."

Retired from Bassett Industries, Hall spends his time

(See Page 2-E, Col. 1)

"All banjo players have their own style, but now everyone wants to imitate Scruggs," he says.
With some coaxing, Hall reminisces on the Mastertone Banjo he sold Scruggs for $150 in 1946.
"If I had it back now I'd make $1,500," he jokes with a bit of trith.

THE EARLIEST KNOWN PHOTOGRAPH OF FLATT AND SCRUGGS ON THEIR OWN. MARCH 1948.

When I was made aware that this photo actually existed, I nearly passed out! This has to be the absolute earliest known photograph of Flatt and Scruggs on their own, as a band in existence! It was taken literally only weeks after they'd departed from Bill Monroe's band, and were trying to form the Foggy Mountain Boys. This is the same photo that was used on the inside cover of the first Foggy Mountain Boys songbook, "Radio Favorites No. 1", printed in 1948. They were already working on station WHKY in Hickory NC, and for that reason they blacked out the "WDVA" on the microphone flag in the photo in the first songbook. I don't believe this photo has ever been printed in its original form elsewhere before now, and I'm very happy to debut it here, in near perfect clarity for the first time. Earl is definitely playing this wonderful RB-75, serial number 518-1. While not only being the earliest known photo of Flatt and Scruggs, it's also the earliest known photo of this banjo in existence. It was only 10 years old, and appears to be in almost new condition. Notice what appears to be a brand new, snow white clean calfskin head, and also that Earl has something written, or engraved on the trussrod cover. I've tried to decipher it, to no avail, even with a 10X loop! Earl's also sporting a ring on his left hand ring finger, even though he and Louise were not married until a few weeks later, on April 18th of that year. I asked Earl about this, and he said it was just a ring he was wearing at the time, and as for the writing on the trussrod cover he couldn't remember exactly what it was, but said it was more than likely his name and address in case the banjo was lost.

The next photo is from a week or so later, after they'd moved to radio station WHKY in Hickory NC, with Earl still playing this banjo. If you'll notice he even has on the same necktie as the WDVA photo! This is an original photo, not a copy. It was culled from the same photography session that produced the famously printed photo featured in the Earl Scruggs instructional book. I don't think this rare original photo has ever been seen or printed anywhere else before now either.

COURTESY THE JIM MILLS COLLECTION

This is a somewhat controversial topic among pre war Gibson banjo enthusiasts that I would like to try and help clear up concerning this banjo if I can... It has been brought to question many times whether this RB-75 serial number 518-1, was in fact the banjo featured on the now legendary first recording of "Foggy Mountain Breakdown". Mr. Scruggs has always stated that he used the RB-Granada on this recording. I would like to clear this up, once and for all, in these pages. **This RB-75 is not the banjo featured on the original 1949 recording of "Foggy Mountain Breakdown".** It was recorded with the RB-Granada, sn 9584-3, that Earl would play for the remainder of his career. I have absolute proof documenting this, which I obtained directly from the late Mr. Benny Sims, fiddle player on this very recording session. Even though it has been mistakenly documented, and printed by several different sources in the past, that this RB-75 was used on this recording, I hope that this will be clear, concise, and perfectly understandable to all who may read it. Mr. Benny Sims was the actual fiddle player on this recording session, and he

COURTESY THE JIM MILLS COLLECTION

FOGGY MOUNTAIN BOYS (L-R) BENNY SIMS, EARL SCRUGGS, CURLY SECKLER, LESTER FLATT AND CEDRIC RAINWATER IN CINNCINATI OHIO STUDIO, DECEMBER 11, 1949. THIS SESSION YIELDED "FOGGY MOUNTAIN BREAKDOWN."

personally provided me with this photograph of the band, taken the very day of this session. This was obviously meant as a promotional photo, with Lester and Earl wearing their riding pants, and was taken inside the recording studios in Cincinnati OH. It appears somewhat posed, but nevertheless according to Sims was taken the same day that they recorded "Foggy Mountain Breakdown". I have absolutely no reason to doubt Mr. Sims whatsoever, as he had "no horse in the race" so to speak, and I'm quite sure that when he told me this years ago, that he couldn't have cared less as to which banjo Earl was playing that day. It's also very clear, as you can see from the afore mentioned photo that Earl is playing the Granada with its original Hearts and Flowers inlay pattern. Earl could not have owned both of these banjos at the same time. You can also follow the time line, and history of this band, along with a complete discography of the "Foggy Mountain Boys" documented very thoroughly in the first Bear Family, Flatt and Scruggs Box set, 1948 to 1959, written by Mr. Neil V. Rosenberg. This details exactly when they started the Foggy Mountain Boys group in March of 1948 at radio station WDVA, in Danville VA, and also when they left for Hickory NC, to work on station WHKY only a few weeks later. They arrived in Bristol, at radio station WCYB, in May of 1948. It also shows that they stayed at WCYB until March of 1949. Earl relayed the story of how he and Don Reno traded banjos "early in 1949", while Flatt and Scruggs were still at Bristol on WCYB. This means they would have without a doubt had to have traded in either, January, February, or March of 1949. This documentation is also now available in the newly updated version of Earl's instructional book "Earl Scruggs and the 5 string banjo", on page 163 and 164. Both Mr. Rosenberg and Earl concur that Flatt and Scruggs definitely left Bristol in March of 1949 for radio station WROL in Knoxville TN, and there is no doubt in my mind that Earl left Bristol with the RB-Granada serial number 9584-3, and not the RB-75 listed here! The first recording of "Foggy Mountain Breakdown" was recorded a whole 9 months later, on December 11th 1949 in Cincinnati OH. The photo of Flatt and Scruggs in the studio with Benny Sims on fiddle, with Earl holding the Granada, is from that very recording session, and as said earlier, I obtained this photo directly from the late Mr. Sims himself. If anyone should know for sure, both he and Earl should, as they were there! I sincerely hope that this clears this story up, once and for all, and plainly shows that this RB-75 serial number 518-1 could not have made this recording, as Earl and Don had already traded banjos long before the Dec. 1949 recording session of FMB ever took place.

Now, back to this RB-75 serial number 518-1, this banjo was already 11 years old, but in nearly new condition when that now legendary trade was made in Bristol VA. It seems that Lester and Earl had invited Bill Monroe to come by the studio at WCYB as a good will gesture, and also to allow him to promote some of his local shows in the area while passing through. Don Reno was playing banjo with Monroe at this time, and Earl had inquired about trading Don for the Granada on previous occasions. Don's problem with trading in the past had been that Earl hadn't yet purchased this RB-75 from Haze Hall, and didn't have a banjo that Reno was willing to trade for. However, when Don saw this RB-75 banjo, he was more than willing to trade, and even threw in a Martin D-18 guitar as boot, because the Granada was in such rough shape, and as said earlier this RB-75 banjo looked almost new. This trade occurred in the studios of WCYB in Bristol, and this accurate account was confirmed again to me by my good friend Dr. Ralph Stanley, who just happened to be standing there in WCYB studios when it all went down. The RB-Granada's serial number is 9584-3, and is also featured in this book. A teenaged Reno had purchased it in 1940, directly from his mentor Snuffy Jenkins.

All of the known photos of Monroe's band which feature Reno on banjo help substantiate the correct time line of this trade, as he is seen already playing this RB-75, and he only worked with Monroe for part of 1948 and 1949. After the trade, Don Reno played and recorded with this RB-75 for most of his career, until his death in 1984. He christened it "Nellie", and also personalized it by carving his name in very small letters in the back of the resonator by the heel cut out, as seen in the close up photos. This banjo has been falsely identified in print many times, as everything from a 1934 RB-3 to an RB-4 by several different individuals.

"DON RENO" CARVED INTO THE BACK OF RESONATOR IN VERY SMALL LETTERS BY DON HIMSELF.

These descriptions were very common, and caused no doubt by the nearly total lack of accurate information available on these banjos in those days. Like I said earlier in the introduction, we have truly grown in leaps and bounds in our knowledge of these wonderful banjos in just the past 10 years or so. Before this time, if it was mahogany it was considered a 3, and if it had a Flying Eagle inlay pattern it was a 4, and that was that.

"DON RENO" WRITTEN INSIDE OF RESONATOR AGAIN BY DON HIMSELF.

As documented earlier, this banjo didn't even ship out of the factory until March of 1938, and it's plainly listed in the featured shipping ledger as RB-75 sn 518-1, so there's absolutely no way possible to accurately call it a 1934 RB-3 or RB-4! I'm not trying to take anything away from anyone's previous writings on this banjo; I'm just trying to get the facts straight once and for all. Again, this is not my opinion; but clear and absolute facts!

This banjo features a somewhat rare inlay pattern for an RB-75, and has since become known to Gibson banjo collectors the world over, as simply the "Reno Pattern". This and a handful of other 75's from this period have this inlay pattern which is actually a Flying Eagle fingerboard inlay, with a style 3/75 peghead inlay, only with the later style "straight across Gibson" inlaid in the peghead. Everything else on this banjo is pretty much late 30's, standard catalog style 75. The Flying Eagle inlay pattern was a throwback to the mid 30's style 4's, and Granada's, and I feel sure that the Gibson Co.

was simply using up left over stock in the fingerboard department. The early 30's period is noted because of the smaller height lettering in the Mastertone blocks on these particular banjos. Nearly every 75 with this "Reno" inlay pattern has the smaller height Mastertone block lettering mainly seen in the early to mid 30's banjos. Take a look at the J D Crowe RB-75, and also the Sonny Osborne Granada featured later in this book. They have this same small lettering in the Mastertone block. Most of the later 75's had a larger block letter pattern seen on several other style 75 banjos featured later in this book from 1937 on. This Reno banjo features a mahogany neck and resonator, nickel plating, and a 20 hole flathead tonering. The serial number was double stamped in this banjo, a practice not that commonly seen. It's easy to see that this rim was stamped with another number ending with a lot number of "2" instead of the "1" that it ended up with. The Mastertone Guarantee Label in this banjo, and another from this same batch of banjos that I have personally inspected with serial number 518, both feature a great rarity because they prove that the Mastertone labels were applied after the tonering was installed at the factory, because the outer black edge of the label runs up off the wood rim and onto the tonering on both banjos, and both little black lines are still very visible today. This is 100% original and very cool!

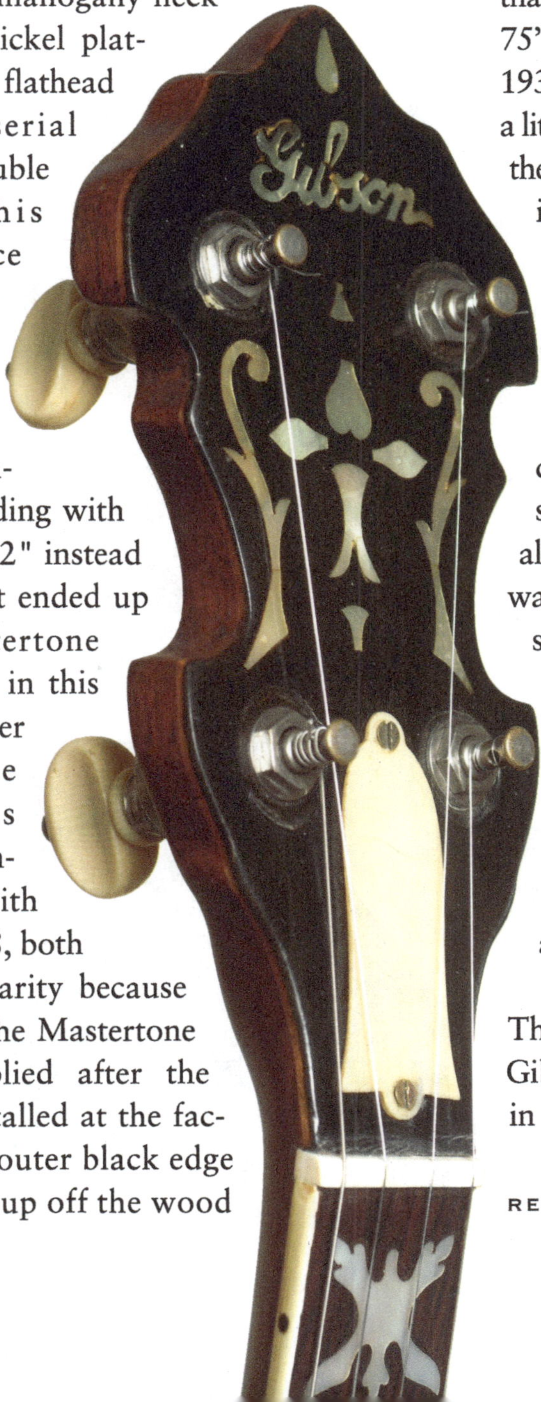

Most of the later style 75's featured slightly taller resonator walls, but several of these early style 75's from 37 and 38 featured the standard size resonators as seen on the mid 30's style 3's. See the Posie Roach, Huber and Mack Crow 75's for the later taller style 75 resonator.

The L-bracket screws in this Reno RB- 75 are still of the flathead variety instead of the Phillips head type, that would be seen just a little while later on most style 75's. As mentioned before, I consider these 75's from 1937 and 38, kind of transitional banjos incorporating a little of the earlier style 3 characteristics with some of the newer style 75 things, such as the same banjo having flathead screws in the L-brackets with Phillips screws in the truss rod cover. Also many of the variations of inlay patterns, different types of neck and resonator wood, and many smaller details were interchanged on the style 75's from this time on. Some folks try to place an exact cutoff date on when the factory supposedly stopped or started this or that particular practice, but that's really impossible to date, because the Gibson factory was just that, a factory, and getting orders filled and shipped out was their main goal, just like any successful factory today. If they ran out of something, they simply used the closest compatible source that was available to complete an order, and ship it out on time. They sure didn't think that anyone would ever be scrutinizing every detail concerning these banjos mfg. nearly 75 years after they left the factory.

This banjo holds the irrefutable title as "The First Gibson Mastertone of Bluegrass", and has survived in very fine condition, with slight restoration to the

RESTORED PEGHEAD OVERLAY.

DOUBLE STAMPED SERIAL NUMBER IN RIM.

FULL UNCUT MASTERTONE LABEL SHOWING BLACK LINE FROM LABEL RIDING UP ONTO THE TONERING.

heel, and peghead overlay. The neck and resonator have been refinished, and it has a slightly damaged flange. At Don's death, the banjo descended to the family. Their youngest son, Don Wayne Reno, was gracious enough to allow us to photograph it for this book, and continues to play this banjo today, and like his Dad, he's a great player also. This RB-75 is definitely one of the most important, and iconic Gibson banjos in the world and still one fine sounding old 75. It has an extremely rich history concerning the earliest development, and incarnation of Bluegrass Music, that will forever be remembered amongst Gibson Flathead Banjo enthusiasts.

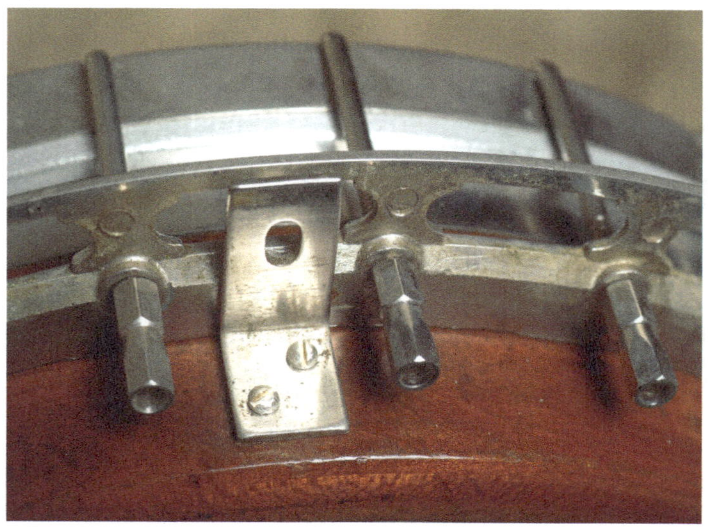

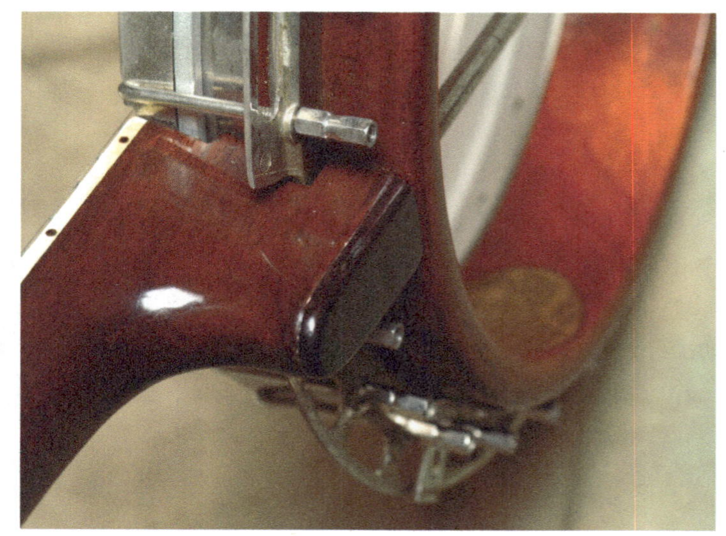

PROVENANCE:

1. Shipped from factory March 9th 1938 to Henry County Furniture Co.
2. First owner Haze Hall, ca.1938 or '39
3. Purchased by Earl Scruggs, ca. 1946
4. Traded to Don Reno, ca. 1949
5. Descended to Mrs. Don Reno, ca. 1984 to date

PEARL MASTERTONE BLOCK SHOWING EARLIER SMALLER TYPE LETTERING

The J. D.Crowe RB-75

SERIAL NUMBER 752-4

The J. D. Crowe RB-75

The first history we have concerning this banjo is that it shipped from the Kalamazoo MI factory June 9th 1938, to Jenkins Music Company in Kansas City MO. This was exactly three months to the day after the "Reno RB-75" also featured in this book, shipped out. It's therefore not so ironic that they both display the same extremely rare inlay pattern featuring a Flying Eagle fingerboard and a style 3/75 peghead inlay. It's also not so ironic then that the "Bill Worrell RB-75" also featured in this book, features an even rarer full Flying Eagle inlay shipped out on October 11th 1937 to this same Jenkins Music Store in K.C. MO.

It seems the factory was using up some of the left over fingerboards from previously produced, but now discontinued models during this 9 month period

The next time this RB-75 serial number 752-4 was to show up to our knowledge was nearly 50 years later in Hot Springs, Arkansas. Even though this banjo's provenance can't be tracked back as long as some listed in this book, it still has one of the most fascinating stories surrounding it that I've ever heard. My good friend J.D. Crowe relayed to me what he knew of this banjos history. This is a most interesting story (almost fairly tale like) of still being able to find an absolute jewel of an Original Flathead RB-75 like this, as late as the mid 1980's, in the most unlikely place you'd ever think of.

"RENO" INLAY PATTERN INCLUDING THE STRAIGHT ACROSS "GIBSON" IN THE PEGHEAD INLAY.

Mr. Bob Rodgers, a banjo player from Little Rock Arkansas, was always on the lookout for most any good vintage quality stringed instrument, when he stumbled upon this banjo while conversing with a friend one day in the summer of 1980. His friend began telling him of a Gibson banjo that he'd recently heard was for sale on a weekly Little Rock Arkansas radio swap shop. The friend said the price was $300.00 and that he was going to take a look at it. All the local radio announcer had said was "Gibson banjo for sale" with a name, and phone number to call. Bob Rodgers told his friend that it was more than likely nothing but a cheap fake parts banjo, or at most something made in the past few years, and that he probably wouldn't really be interested in it, but to let him know after he'd seen it. A few days later Mr. Rodgers' friend returned with this 1938, RB-75, Original Flathead Fivestring, serial number 752-4, in nearly mint condition! It seems the lady who'd answered the phone's late husband had owned the banjo, and she had decided to put it up for sale, and simply ran an ad on her local weekly radio swap shop, and Mr. Rodgers' friend had just purchased it. Well to put it mildly Bob Rodgers just couldn't believe it, and really wanted this banjo badly!

My God, who wouldn't?

Luckily for Bob it turned out that the new owner of the banjo, his friend, didn't really care for the flathead type of tone in a banjo, and preferred the archtop sound of Ralph Stanley. When Mr. Rodgers went to his home to try and make a trade with him on a 1928 TB-3 fivestring conversion, his friend wasn't against trading at all, and actually liked Bob's banjo so much that he offered Bob this Original Flathead RB-75 and $50.00 boot for his banjo!! The only problem was that his friend wanted to swap resonators on the two banjos. He actually wanted to keep this original RB-75's resonator!!!

Bob proceeded to try and talk some sense into this guy, but he was a well known alcoholic and pretty tough to reason with most of the time, so Bob said listen, I'll make a deal with you...I'll trade with you and give you $100.00 boot if I can keep the original resonator.

That $100.00 bill sealed the deal, and in the year 1980, Bob Rodgers brought home this fine specimen of an Original Flathead Fivestring RB-75 for a $100.00 bill, plus a 1928 two piece flange TB-3 five-string conversion banjo in trade.

Bob, being good friends with J.D. Crowe, told Crowe of his wonderful find, but it would be a good while before Crowe would actually get to see it. While working on a tour with the "Bluegrass Album Band" flying across America in 1983, the airline broke the neck on J.D.'s banjo, and a replacement had to be found quickly. J.D. remembered his old friend Bob Rodgers and called on him in the time of need. Bob was glad to oblige by bringing this RB-75 to the show that night for Crowe to play.

J.D. told me upon first seeing this banjo that he thought it was a newer copy or a fake! He said it was so clean and just in almost perfect condition. Then upon closer examination he noticed the smaller sized, factory original frets, friction 5th peg, and just everything it was supposed to have. He couldn't believe it!

J.D. told Bob Rodgers that if he let him play this banjo for the rest of the tour, that he was going to have to fly with it, and Bob said "Ah hell J.D. play it! It's just a banjo; if it breaks we'll fix it"! Well, the rest is history, as Crowe soon fell in love with this banjo, and told Bob Rodgers, "You're not getting it back"! Bob told J.D. to just keep it, and play it as long as he wanted too.

After several years of playing and recording with it, J.D. decided he truly did not want to part with this banjo, and he and Bob were able to come to an agreement on price, and J.D. has owned and played the banjo every since 1990. This banjo and every other with this serial number that are accounted for are all original flathead fivestring RB-75's. They also all feature the rare "Reno" inlay pattern. This is identified by a Flying Eagle fingerboard, with a style 3 or 75 peghead inlay. The only difference is the "Gibson" in the peghead was inlaid in a straight line rather than at a slant as on most with this peghead inlay.

Don Reno's RB-75, also featured in this book, is from the serial number batch of 518, and every banjo known in this lot are all inlaid, and appointed exactly the same as this batch of serial number 752. It has been published many times by different people that these non catalog standard inlay patterns were a custom option, but this really has no founding whatsoever, as it makes absolutely no sense at all that **every banjo known in both of these serial number ranges 752 and 518 would be custom ordered exactly alike.** Speaking of the batch of identical RB-75's in the 752 series with the same inlay pattern, here's a photo of an exact mate to Crowe's banjo, it's RB-75, serial number 752-2, and belongs to a good friend of mine and Crowe's, Mr. Jerry Keys of East TN, who has owned it for many years now. The fellow in the photograph with the banjo is the original owner, Mr. Thomas Martin, and this photo was taken at radio station WGRV in Greeneville TN, in 1946. He appears to be playing in the newly popular 3 fingered style and also has an original factory headguard on the banjo. The band was called "Carl Sauceman and the Greene Valley Boy's".

COURTESY THE JERRY KEYS COLLECTION

In reality no one can explain why all these banjos were produced with this higher grade inlay pattern in the fingerboard, other than by deducing that a Gibson factory worker was simply using up left over stock in the fingerboard department, and just happened to choose these two serial number batches of style 75, to use them up on. It's also worth noting that by the 1937-38 period, when these banjos were being produced, that there was no current model banjo being manufactured that featured this Flying Eagle fingerboard inlay, so they were useless other than being used up on these lower grade style 75 banjos.

The Flying Eagle pattern had long been reserved for the higher grade style 4, and Granada banjos, which were both discontinued in 1937 with the advent of the newer top tension design. The newly designated budget model Mastertone, style 75, which had previously been called the style 3, was introduced at $75.00, where as the style 3 had been priced at $100.00. This gave the factory a means to use up any leftover part from any other standard, non toptension model banjo on these budget model 75's after 1937. Check out the Bill Worrell RB-75, featured in this book, for a rare full Flying Eagle inlaid style 75. Anything left at the factory that was usable was fair game it seems, and was freely used to complete these new budget model style 75's, especially in the later years leading into WWII.

To further prove this, my good friend Jerry Keys has allowed us to reprint for the first time these extremely rare, original factory documents that show the Government was severely cutting back the Gibson Company's total production and is dated March 15th 1942. The other is a "Limitation Order" and it's dated June 17th 1942. It's also signed by Gibson's General Manager, Mr. Guy Hart. It was sent stapled inside the "BB" catalog of 1942 titled……"To All Gibson Dealers".

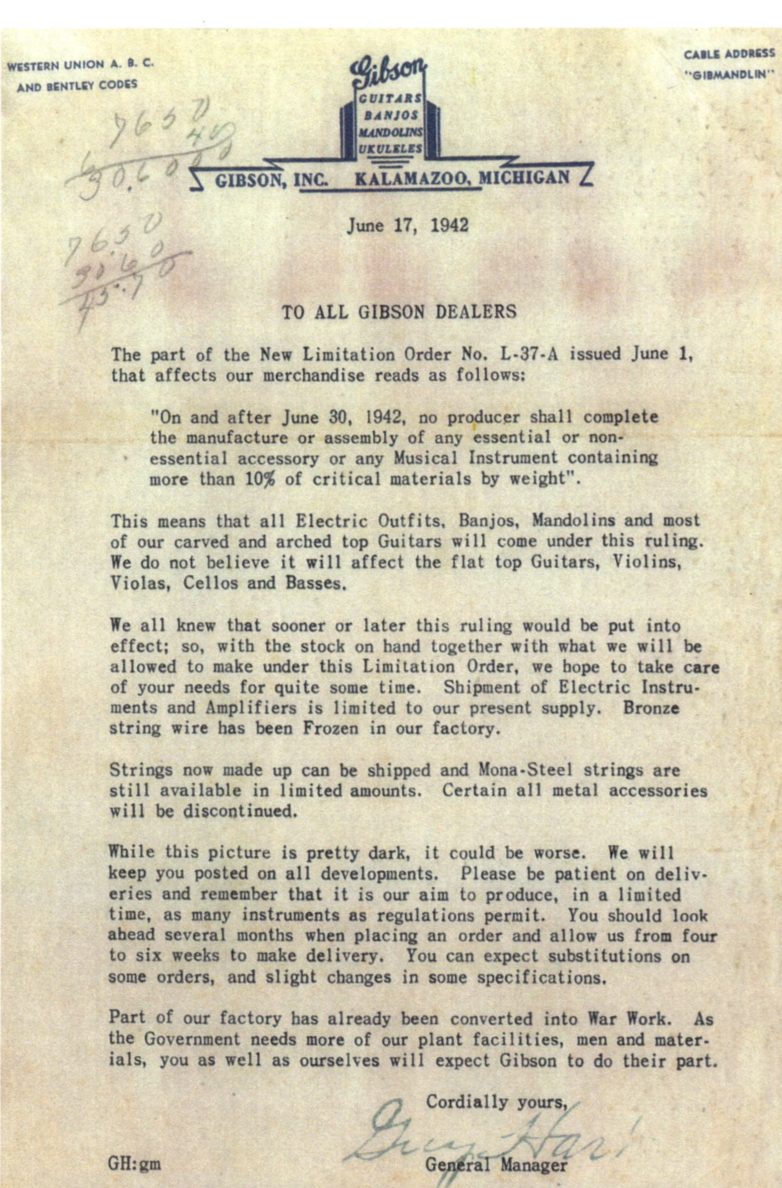

WESTERN UNION A. B. C. AND BENTLEY CODES

CABLE ADDRESS "GIBMANDLIN"

Gibson GUITARS BANJOS MANDOLINS UKULELES

GIBSON, INC. KALAMAZOO, MICHIGAN

June 17, 1942

TO ALL GIBSON DEALERS

The part of the New Limitation Order No. L-37-A issued June 1, that affects our merchandise reads as follows:

"On and after June 30, 1942, no producer shall complete the manufacture or assembly of any essential or non-essential accessory or any Musical Instrument containing more than 10% of critical materials by weight".

This means that all Electric Outfits, Banjos, Mandolins and most of our carved and arched top Guitars will come under this ruling. We do not believe it will affect the flat top Guitars, Violins, Violas, Cellos and Basses.

We all knew that sooner or later this ruling would be put into effect; so, with the stock on hand together with what we will be allowed to make under this Limitation Order, we hope to take care of your needs for quite some time. Shipment of Electric Instruments and Amplifiers is limited to our present supply. Bronze string wire has been Frozen in our factory.

Strings now made up can be shipped and Mona-Steel strings are still available in limited amounts. Certain all metal accessories will be discontinued.

While this picture is pretty dark, it could be worse. We will keep you posted on all developments. Please be patient on deliveries and remember that it is our aim to produce, in a limited time, as many instruments as regulations permit. You should look ahead several months when placing an order and allow us from four to six weeks to make delivery. You can expect substitutions on some orders, and slight changes in some specifications.

Part of our factory has already been converted into War Work. As the Government needs more of our plant facilities, men and materials, you as well as ourselves will expect Gibson to do their part.

Cordially yours,

Guy Hart

General Manager

GH:gm

COURTESY THE JERRY KEYS COLLECTION

This all important piece of documentation regarding all of the later manufactured Mastertone banjos comes from the personal collection of my good friend Mr. Jerry Keys, and I want to thank him again for allowing us to reproduce it here for the first time.

These documents basically stated that the Government had issued a "limitation order" and that Gibson was being forced to cut back on production, and several models of instruments may have different features other than what was listed in their catalog descriptions, because of shortage of materials due to the War effort. It also explains the mandatory orders they have from the Government forcing them to cut their total production. It states that any instruments with a "critical material mass of 25% or more" may be cut by as much as 50% of their total production of 1940 totals which were already extremely low to begin with.

Banjos being half nuts and bolts just happen to have the highest amount of "critical material" in all of Gibson's line of musical instruments.

I truly have to believe that the Gibson factory had been secretly dealing with these government cutbacks long before these featured documents were made public, (read between the lines in the Guy Hart letter: "We all knew that sooner or later this ruling would be put into effect") I think that no one really knew which way the War in Europe was going to turn until this time, and I also feel sure that the Government had been in contact with most major Manufacturing plants throughout the U.S. for quite some time preceding this, in case things should change for the worse on the war front. This would clearly explain the many variations of the style 75's and also toptensions that we see today made from approx. 1939 on, when things were really starting to heat up in Europe. I've seen just about every configuration of these banjos that you can imagine... mahogany resonators with maple necks, maple resonators and walnut necks, and style 75's with left over walnut style 4 resonators with concentric wood purfling, mismatched plating's and parts in general. This is why I see the style 75 as the most interesting of all the pre war Mastertones, as so many different variations were produced up until the end of banjo production during WWII.

Back to this fine RB-75, serial number 752-4. J.D. has played this banjo and a few others he owns for several years now, but has kept this banjo in very fine condition. He's had a Frank Neat exact replica neck on it for years, while playing it on the road, but has graciously put it back to as close to the original specs as possible. He installed the original neck and tuners, just for me to reproduce in this book, and I want to thank him kindly for going to the trouble. As noted in the Reno RB-75, also featured in this book, the lettering in the Mastertone block is of the small type not found typically on this late a banjo.

The original frets are another consideration worth mentioning. All the completely original examples that I've seen from both these batches of "Reno" inlaid banjo's, that still had their original frets intact, had the small gauge of fret wire mainly seen prior to 1937. It leads me to believe that these necks were possibly completed a few years prior to the banjos even being finished and shipped out, or the fingerboards were already completely made up, fretted, and lying around, and then were simply glued onto these necks as these two batches (518 & 752) were being assembled. One more anomaly associated with this particular banjo, is the placement of the Mastertone Guarantee label inside of the rim. It's on the top side of the rim directly beside the serial number stamping. The Mastertone labels were normally placed on the opposite side of the rim from the serial number stamping.

WE ARE FORCED TO CUT PRODUCTION

The government has issued orders that musical instrument production be reduced from 25% to 50%, based on the weight of critical materials used in each instrument. The principal critical materials are iron, steel, aluminum, tin, nickel, lead, zinc, copper, and rubber.

Instruments with less than 10% critical materials are cut to 75% of our 1940 production --- this includes arch top and flat top guitars; mandolins, ukuleles and the violin family of instruments.

Instruments using 10% and less than 25% critical materials are cut to 65% of our 1940 production.

Items containing 25% or more critical materials are cut 50% -- this includes all electric outfits; all banjos.

(See Other Side)

The order went into effect March 1st, and unfortunately our volume is based on what was done in 1940 -- not 1941.

Articles considered as replacement and repair items are cut to 75% of 1940 total. This includes strings, picks, music stands, cases, bows and other accessories.

This program contains no guarantee that manufacturers can secure raw materials even in reduced quantities.

By eliminating certain critical materials, substituting where possible and cutting the amounts used on each instrument, we can make more instruments without affecting the tone, quality and serviceability.

GIBSON, INC., Kalamazoo, Mich. March 15, 1942

COURTESY THE JERRY KEYS COLLECTION

Again this is just another little indicator that should show us all that no one can say... "they absolutely only did it this way or that way from the factory originally" in the 1930's and 40's.

In any event this is one great RB-75, with an uncut label, 20 hole flathead tonering, nickel plating, and mahogany neck and resonator. Totally standard catalog style 75, except for the rare "Reno" style inlay pattern.

J. D. Crowe has done a great service by playing and promoting Pre War Gibson Flathead Banjo's for over 50 years now , and also by allowing the Gibson Co. to replicate this RB-75 as close as possible, to create the "J. D. Crowe model RB-75". This is one of Gibson's best sellers currently, and is also a fine newer banjo.

Thanks to Mr. J. D. Crowe for his main contribution....recording some of the absolute best Bluegrass banjo playing ever, for all of us to follow on a powerful Original Fivestring Flathead Mastertone Banjo!

J.D. CROWE

COURTESY GIBSON INC.

PERFECT UNCUT MASTERTONE LABEL IN A RARE LOCATION CLOSE TO THE SERIAL NUMBER,THIS IS THE OPPOSITE SIDE OF WHERE THEY ARE NORMALLY SEEN.

SERIAL NUMBER IN CHALK ONLY IN RESONATOR.

PROVENANCE:

1. Shipped June 9th, 1938 to Jenkins Music Company of Kansas City MO.
2. Purchased by its first owner, possibly a Mr. LeBiles listed in the shipping ledger.
3. Unknown whereabouts for approx. 42 years until it turns up in Hot Springs, Arkansas on a radio swap shop for sale in 1980.
4. Purchased by Bob Rodgers friend directly off an Arkansas radio swap shop for $300.00 in 1980.
5. Purchased by Bob Rodgers three months later in 1980.
6. Purchased by present owner J. D. Crowe in 1990.

RARE ORIGINAL 5 STRING TENSION HOOP, AND MASTERTONE BLOCK WITH SMALLER HEIGHT LETTERING.

The Posie Roach RB-75

SERIAL NUMBER EA-5691

The Posie Roach RB-75

The first recorded history we have on this banjo is that it shipped out of Gibson's Kalamazoo MI plant, May 10th 1940, to Henry County Furniture Co. of Martinsville Virginia.

Just two years earlier in 1938, this very same store sold the Don Reno RB-75, "Nellie" also featured in this book, when it was brand new. It was not uncommon in that day for furniture stores, jewelry stores, and other types of businesses to sell musical instruments, as there were very few true music stores in the rural south. This RB-75, serial number EA-5691, was purchased new in 1940. Its first owner's name is unknown, but thanks to the second owners early insight we do have the second date of purchase written inside the resonator in pencil. He purchased it only a year later, on September 3rd 1941 as can be seen in these photos. Mr. Posie Roach Sr., of Axton Va. gave $100.00 and a cheaper banjo in trade for this RB-75 serial number EA-5691. It was only a year old and like new. Mr. Roach was a well known musician in the surrounding area of Martinsville VA, and owned and played this banjo for nearly 60 years, until his death in 2000. He was 88 years old. The banjo descended to his son, Posie Roach Jr., and was purchased from him by the author in 2003.

"P. L. ROACH SEPT. 3RD 1941" PURCHASE DATE, PENCILED INSIDE WALL OF RESONATOR BY MR. ROACH HIMSELF.

This RB-75 had traveled less than 15 miles from where it was purchased brand new, nearly 63 years earlier.

The banjo is 100% original as the day it left the factory. It has the normal wear expected from 60 years of being played. It has the standard late 75 inlay pattern, full uncut Mastertone label, original friction fifth peg and both bone nuts, Rogers calfskin head, 20 hole flathead tonering, serial number stamped into the back of the peghead, and original redline case with the wrench. It also features its original Gibson hang tag, instructional papers from the factory on setup, case key in the original factory envelope, the original 2 foot bridge, and a box of Gibson banjo strings from the 40's.

It also still retains its original Kluson amber button tuners. This is another thing that collectors and scholars use to date certain Gibson banjos even ones

SERIAL NUMBER STAMPED INTO BACK OF PEGHEAD, AND KLUSON AMBER BUTTON TUNERS,

ORIGINAL HANG TAG, AMBER BUTTON 5TH STRING FRICTION PEG, AND ORIGINAL NUT.

without serial numbers. It seems no one knows exactly when the Gibson Company started using Kluson tuners in place of the Grover tuners they had previously been using for nearly a decade and a half. You start seeing the Kluson Amber buttoned tuners around 1938 and after, although you still see Grover tuners used occasionally after this time also. There were two distinctly different styles of amber buttoned Kluson banjo tuners and both of these are photographed in this book. The 1st type are featured on this Posie Roach RB-75, and the 2nd type are the so called "stairstep" design mainly used on toptension banjos. They are pictured on the RB-7 featured in this book. The only thing non catalog standard about this banjo is the chrome-plated tonering, and L brackets. It's very common to find 100% factory original banjos with more than one type of plating being used on the same banjo at this time. It seems to be found mostly among E, EA, F, and FA serial numbered RB-75's, and many Toptensions from this period. This was due to a shortage of materials during this period leading up to WWII. Another odd thing some folks may see in the photo of the inside of the resonator is where it appears that someone wiped another serial number out and wrote in 5691. This is exactly what happened, at the factory in 1940!! If you look at the number closely you'll see that it's 5101. This is the serial number of another completely original RB-75, exactly like this one in every way, which left the factory at approximately the same time and almost ended up with this banjos resonator! My friend Glen Rose of TN owns this very banjo, RB-75 serial number FA-5101, and it's a fine example as well. It seems that factory workers possibly had these two banjos laid out on the bench for assembly at the same time, and a factory worker nearly paired this resonator with the wrong banjo! He then wiped his mistake out with his hand and wrote the correct number 5691 in the resonator where both have existed for nearly

CORRECT SERIAL NUMBER 5691 IN CHALK INSIDE RESONATOR, BUT ALSO SHOWS SERIAL NUMBER 5101 WRITTEN BY MISTAKE IN SAME HAND AND SMEARED OUT BY FACTORY WORKER.

LATER LARGER KNURLED THUMBSCREWS, AND RARE FACTORY ORIGINAL CHROME PLATED TONERING.

70 years now. I've actually owned several other all original pre war Gibson banjos over the years with this same near mistake still visible inside them. Curtis McPeake and I recently dismantled this banjo to weigh the tonering, and discovered that it's nearly identical in cut and weight to his old RB-75 "Betsy", also featured in this book.

COURTESY THE JIM MILLS COLLECTION

"Betsy" has an original chrome-plated tonering as well. It's serial number F906-1, and is a very fine sounding banjo, as is the "Posie Roach" RB-75 serial number EA-5691.

I've never really cleaned this old banjo up completely, and I would say that it still retains a lot of Mr. Roach's DNA on it, as you can see in the photos. I don't know why I've left it with all its original old dirt and grime intact, I guess it just looked right to me. The fingerboard has never been dressed, and most of the frets are still original.

When you really clean these old banjos up, dress the fingerboards down, re fret them, replace the friction 5th string tuners, and change both of the original nuts, etc... they lose a lot of their original old pre war patina, look, and character.

This one still retained it all, so I left it alone.

Here's a great photo that came in the case with the banjo. It's of Mr. Roach playing at the National Guard Building in Martinsville VA. in 1942, very soon after acquiring this fine RB-75.

I recently recorded the title track of my newest CD, on Sugar Hill Records, "Hide Head Blues" with this banjo, and I've probably had more compliments on the tone of this one banjo than all the rest on the record. I think it's partly due to the 1930's Joseph Rogers calfskin head, combined with that original chrome plated Flathead Tonering. It could have just been the right conditions in the studio that particular day, I really don't know, but I'll have to say it recorded just wonderful. I'm very thankful to get to own and play such a fine banjo.

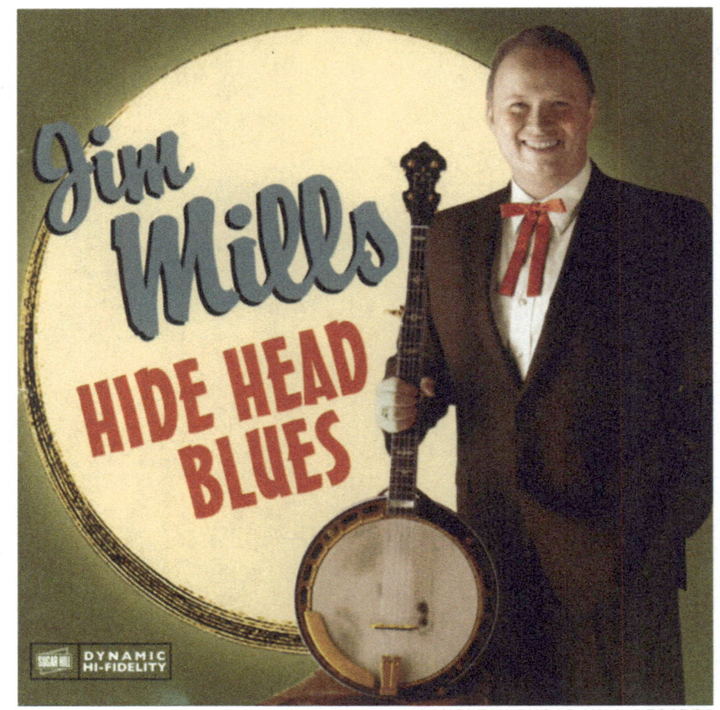

COURTESY SUGAR HILL RECORDS

PROVENANCE:

1. Shipped out of the Gibson factory, in Kalamazoo MI, May 10th, 1940
2. Retailed by Henry County Furniture Co., of Martinsville VA ca. 1940
3. Purchased by original owner, name is unknown, ca. 1940
4. Purchased by Posie Roach Sr., from original owner, Sept. 3rd, 1941
5. Descended to Posie Roach Jr., ca. 2000
6. Purchased by Jim Mills, Nov. 2003

TYPICAL STYLE 75 INLAY PATTERN IN DOUBLE CUT PEGHEAD.

ORIGINAL 5 STRING TENSIONHOOP, AND PEARL MASTERTONE BLOCK SHOWING LARGER LATER STYLE HIGH PROFILE LETTERING,

The Curtis McPeake RB-75
"Ole Betsy"
SERIAL NUMBER F906-1

The Curtis McPeake RB-75 "Ole Betsy"

This banjos original shipping ledger indicates that it left the factory April 9th 1941, and was shipped directly to Mr. L. B. Cowen of Gordonsville TN. Many banjos such as this one never made it to a dealer because they were purchased directly from the factory, paid for in full, and then shipped to their new owner, never going through a music store. Several were sold at the factory direct and therefore never even made it into the shipping ledgers. Mr. Cowen owned this banjo for 17 years, until 1958 when he sold it to my good friend and world renowned pre war Gibson banjo scholar Curtis McPeake, who has owned and played it for nearly 50 years now. Mr. McPeake has told me the story of its purchase many times, and it's a classic that I never tire of hearing. Curtis was working with Bill Monroe and his Bluegrass Boy's at the time, and also filling in for Earl Scruggs when needed. While working in Monroe's band he befriended guitar player Jimmy Maynard, who told him about a gentleman who lived close to him that had an older Gibson Mastertone. Curtis said that he had known about the banjo existing, and had an idea of where it was located for a good long while before actually going to take a look at it and to see if it could be bought. All he knew was that it was a Gibson Mastertone. He told me it didn't really matter all that much because in the 1950's, he didn't have the funds to think about purchasing something that expensive most of the time anyway. Several months later, on a pretty Sunday afternoon Curtis and his wife decided to take a Sunday drive and ended up close to where this fellow with the banjo's farm was supposed to be. Curtis told his wife "let's go see if we can find that banjo"! He asked a neighbor for directions to Mr. Cowen's farm, and was directed just a few miles down the road. When Curtis arrived at the house he was greeted by Mr. Cowen's wife, and when he introduced himself and asked about a banjo that may be for sale she told him that her husband wasn't at home right now, but that he did have a banjo, and she proceeded to bring it out onto the porch! Curtis said when he opened the case, he knew immediately what he was looking at, and was shocked by its condition, nearly mint! Mrs. Cowen told Curtis that her husband was working on the farm, less than a mile or so away, and to drive down and talk with him concerning the banjo. Curtis left the banjo at the house and went to see Mr. Cowen. He arrived and found him working in a field with his father. Curtis introduced himself to Mr. Cowen and his father, explained why he was there, and asked

STANDARD STYLE 75 INLAY WITH ADDED INLAY AROUND TUNERS AND VERY TOP, ALSO CAM STYLE D-TUNERS, AND SMALLER BELL SHAPED TRUSSROD COVER WITH PHILLIPS SCREWS.

if his banjo was for sale. Mr. Cowen looked kind of puzzled as to what to do, and asked his dad "what do you think I should do"? Curtis said that this made him mighty uneasy, and he then wished that maybe he'd waited later to try and do business. Fortunately, the father said, "son you don't ever play the thing, why don't you just sell it to this man". Breathing a sigh of relief, Curtis then asked him, what would you have to have for it? Mr. Cowen

SERIAL NUMBER IN CHALK ON RESONATOR, WITH TWO LARGER KNURL THUMBSCREWS AND TWO WITH SMALLER KNURLS.

answered "well I couldn't take any less than $100.00 for it". Curtis said he didn't want to look overly excited and offered him $75.00 just to make it look good, to which Mr. Cowen quickly declined, so then Curtis agreed to purchase this wonderful RB-75 for One Single Ben Franklin! Its serial number F906-1, which has over the last 50 years, simply become known as "Ole Betsy".

Although Curtis said that Mr. Cowen told him he'd purchased this banjo new in the late 1930's, the shipping ledgers don't lie, and I am convinced that the shipping date of 1941 is correct, as the overall features of this particular banjo are more in line with this later date. People give me dates all the time concerning when they think something was bought or sold sometime back over 40 years ago, and often after further research, their recollections are usually off by a few years. After so much time has passed it's very easy to miscalculate by only a year or two. I know I can hardly remember what I had for lunch yesterday! So it's often a case of simply being mistaken about a certain year or linking it mistakenly with some other event that happened long ago. This RB-75 doesn't conform exactly to standard catalog specs. It features the standard pot construction of a style 75 with mahogany resonator, and nickel plated metal, that is except for the original high profile 20 hole flathead tonering. The tonering came from the factory chrome plated, and is 100% original. (This is also seen on the Posie Roach RB-75 featured in this book) The banjo also has a gold plated tail bracket which Curtis said came on it originally, so he

ORIGINAL GOLD PLATED TAILPIECE HANGER AND NUT.

just left it. It makes perfect sense that this banjo shipped out in the 1940's, as at this time the Gibson Company was using up all left over parts, and the budget model 75 was the best place to get rid of them. Several toptensions from this same period are also known to be totally original that were made up using parts from 2 or 3 different models of the period, and often have more than one type of plating's on different parts, and different wood types in the resonator and neck. Also mismatched bindings are occasionally encountered.

This RB-75 serial number F906-1, features a maple neck with a volute, or hand stop, with the serial number stamped in the back of the peghead. Many RB-75's that feature a maple neck don't have hand stops at all, see "The Last RB-75" featured in this book for reference. If you'll also notice on the later style 75's featured in this book with letter prefixes, and serial numbers stamped into the back of the peghead, such as this McPeake banjo, the Posie Roach, the Steve Huber, and the Mack Crow, you'll notice the hand stops feature a somewhat "wider smile" than the earlier known examples such as the Bill Worrell, the Reno, and the J. D. Crowe 75's which have a "tighter smile" as seen on most earlier 1930's style 3's.

This banjo has had some extra inlay added in fret positions 19 and 22, and also some added inlay in the peghead years ago. Curtis also had Walt Pittman of California install a set of his cam type D-tuners in the 1960's. The pearl Mastertone block at the 21st fret seems to have a later style "Mastertone" engraved as it's a postwar style engraving. Other than this the banjo is 100% original and in excellent overall condition. It features a full uncut Mastertone label, Kluson amber button tuners, and the wider knurls on the thumbscrews only seen on these later produced banjos. It's one of the finest sounding flatheads I've played, and Curtis is a master at getting the best out of it. We all owe Mr. Curtis McPeake a great debt of gratitude for not only keeping the flame burning, but also for sharing his knowledge and furthering the interest overall in these fine old banjos for the past 40 years or more.

Thanks Curtis.....

BACK OF PEGHEAD SHOWING KLUSON AMBER BUTTON TUNERS WITH SERIAL NUMBER STAMPED INTO BACK, ALSO SHOWING HAND STOP ON AN ORIGINAL MAPLE NECK, WHICH IS A RARITY.

PROVENANCE:

1. Shipped from the factory April 9th 1941 to L. B. Cowen

2. Purchased by present owner, Curtis McPeake in 1958

Post Script: Since the time of this writing, a consecutively serial numbered, exact mate to this McPeake RB-75 has surfaced that was previously completely unknown to the pre war Gibson banjo community. It had remained in the original owners family all these years, still 100% original, and is identical in every way to the McPeake banjo except it has a nickel plated 20 hole flathead tonering rather than the chrome. It even features the same gold plated tail bracket! This banjo is serial number F906-2. It shipped from the factory Feb. 10th 1941. It was sold through George Gruhn to my good friend and great banjo player Charlie Cushman in late 2007.

FACTORY ORIGINAL CHROME PLATED TONERING.

PERFECT UNCUT MASTERTONE LABEL.

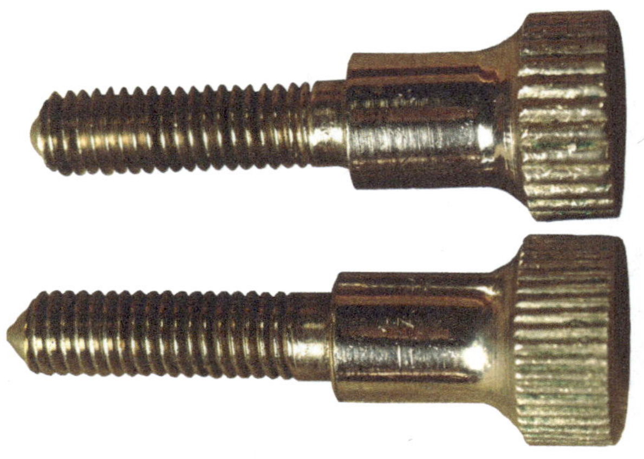

ORIGINAL 5 STRING TENSIONHOOP, AND PEARL MASTERTONE BLOCK SHOWING LATER POST WAR STYLE LETTERING, AND ADDED DIAMOND FINGERBOARD INLAY.

The Steve Huber RB-75

SERIAL NUMBER FA-5004

The Steve Huber RB-75

This banjo is one of the very few that survive today complete with its "Original Bill of Sale". It shipped out of the factory on January 30th 1940 to Walburg and Auge, believed to have been a hardware store in Worchester MA. The photo of its original bill of sale proves that this banjo came originally with a #522 silk plush lined hard shell case from the factory which were quite rare and expensive. These cases were priced in the Gibson catalog at $22.00 where the standard #521 flannel lined cases were priced at only $14.50. With the addition of the deluxe case, and the $82.50 price of the banjo itself, with taxes the total came to $106.50!

THIS BILL SUBJECT TO SIGHT DRAFT AT 30 DAYS FROM DATE WITHOUT NOTICE.

WALBERG & AUGE

31 MERCANTILE ST. - 86 MECHANIC ST.

WORCESTER, MASS.

Shipped via — Terms, Cash

Your Order — Date Feb 3, 1940.

Sold to . Mr. Leon D. Warren,

16 Water St.,

Whitinsville, Mass.

WHEN PAYING BY CHECK PLEASE DETACH AND MAIL THIS STUB WITH CHECK. YOUR CANCELLED CHECK IS YOUR RECEIPT. AMOUNT OF CHECK $

	ACCOUNT RENDERED	
1	#RB75 5string Gibson banjo	82.50
1	#522 Plush lined case for same	24.00
		106.50

PAID

FEB - 3 1940

WALBERG & AUGE

BY

WALBERG & AUGE, WORCESTER, MASS. DATE RENDERED 19

A. E. MARTELL CO., KEENE, N. H.

COURTESY STEVE HUBER

EXTREMELY RARE ORIGINAL BILL OF SALE.

As can be seen from the bill of sale photo, Mr. Leon Warren purchased this banjo on February 3rd 1940, only 4 days after it shipped from the factory. If I had to speculate, I would say it was more than likely ordered for Mr. Warren by Walberg & Auge, as he paid for it in full that day. Most of the banjos still found with their original bills of sale show that they were paid for "on time" with a minimal down payment, and then finishing with monthly payments. On page 118 is a photo of a similar period bill of sale from an original PB-18 courtesy of my good friend Darrell McCumbers. This original bill of sale shows the down payment, and also how the monthly payments were broken up.

Back to this RB-75 serial number FA-5004. This is an extremely rare example that features the only known neck with this particular configuration. Factory original maple necked RB-75's with mahogany resonators are not uncommon, but this one not only has an interesting inlay pattern, it features a toptension peghead design, and handstop. Basically it's an RB-7 style toptension neck, but features style 75 stain color and finish, as well as a flat, non arched fingerboard, proving that it definitely came originally on this banjo without a doubt.

5 bar 3.60

To APP'S MUSIC HOUSE (Name of Dealer)
BURLINGTON, IOWA (City and State)

No.
Date Aug. 21, 1941

(C) Cash Price	$ 225.00
(D) Down Payment	$ 145.00
Cash Balance	$ 80.00
(S) Service Chg.	$ 3.60
(T) Time Balance	$ 83.60

Undersigned acknowledges delivery and acceptance of One PB Gibson Banjo & Case Model PB-18 Serial No. ______ for which I promise to pay you or your order the sum of (C) + (S) Two hundred twenty-eight and 60/100------------ Dollars ($228.60), as follows: (D) $100.00 in cash herewith; Trade in $45.00, and balance of (T) $ 83.60 payable to the order of above named seller, his or its successors or assigns, at the time or times stated in the schedule of payments set forth hereon:

Schedule of Payments

Due Date	Amt.	Due Date	Amt.
Sep 3	$4.63	Mar 3	$4.63
Sep 18	$4.63	Mar 18	$4.63
Oct 3	$4.63	Apr 3	$4.63
Oct 18	$4.63	Apr 18	$4.63
Nov 3	$4.63	May 3	$4.63
Nov 18	$4.63	May 18	$4.89
Dec 3	$4.63		$
Dec 18	$4.63		$
Jan 3	$4.63		$
Jan 18	$4.63		$
Feb 3	$4.63		$
Feb 18	$4.63		$

In case of failure to make any payment in the time and manner as herein provided, the entire unpaid balance of the purchase price, shall, at the option of the seller, his or its order or assigns, become immediately due and payable, without notice or demand, said notice and demand being hereby expressly waived, and the purchaser agrees to make such payments, in default of which, the seller, his or its assigns may, at their option, retake said property without legal process, except that nothing in this agreement shall be construed as obligating the seller to accept return of said property in lieu of purchase price agreed to be paid, but in the event of such re-taking any amount that may have been paid thereon shall be considered as payment for use, ordinary wear, and depreciation of said property while in the possession of the purchaser, and in the absence of provision of law to the contrary, shall be retained by seller. If the amount so paid shall not cover the reasonable rental value and depreciation of said property, the purchaser agrees to pay seller on demand the balance of such amount.

Undersigned purchaser agrees that a collection or attorney fee of 10% of the principal sum above mentioned or such amount as may appear to be unpaid thereon, shall become due and payable on default in any payment at maturity, and consents that such fee shall be made a part of any judgment rendered hereon. Purchaser does further promise and agree that if the contract be sold or assigned by the seller herein, and thereafter by reason of default herein on the part of the purchaser, the seller shall repurchase or take up said contract from such buyer and thereby suffer any loss or expense he, purchaser, herein, will pay such loss or expense with interest, and hereby agrees that the amount of such loss or expense may be made a part of the purchase price and a part of any judgment hereon.

The purchaser for himself and his successors in interest hereby waives, so far as is consistent with public policy the benefits of any exemptions of this State, and any causes of action thereunder. Any part of this agreement contrary to the laws of this State shall not invalidate the other parts of this instrument.

It is agreed title to the above described property and all material and parts furnished in connection therewith shall not pass to the purchaser until the price thereof, or any judgment for all or part of the same, is paid in full, and that until such payment said property and parts shall remain the property of said seller, his or its successors or assigns. Until full performance of this contract, the undersigned agrees not to remove said property from the place of original delivery without first obtaining written consent of the holder of this contract. Undersigned agrees to pay all taxes on said Property, and to complete payment if the Property is lost, stolen, damaged or destroyed, against which contingencies purchaser agrees to keep said property insured.

It is understood and agreed that this contract cannot be cancelled, and no other agreement, or guarantee, verbal, written or implied, shall limit or qualify the terms of this contract.

Executed in triplicate, one copy of which was delivered to and retained by the purchaser, this 21st day of August, 1941

Accepted:
(Dealer)

Signed Delbert C Wasson (Purchaser)

Witness:
Salesman
Street or Rural Address
City and State

DEALER'S COPY.
Acres-Blackmar Co., Burlington. 16742

COURTESY DARRELL McCUMBERS

1941, ORIGINAL "BILL OF SALE" FOR A PB-18 PAID OFF ON TIME.

trussrod cover which were common on many style 75 banjos from this late period. The thumb screws are also of the later wide knurl variety, and can be seen on a few other 1940's produced banjos such as the Mack Crow RB-75, and also the Curtis McPeake RB-75 in this book.

Steve found this banjo in a Pennsylvania music store in the mid 1980's. He ended up paying $5000.00 plus allowing a 1950's Martin D-28 guitar for it in trade. This was a very good trade even at this time, as the going rate for a typical Flathead Fivestring Mastertone at this time in America was around $12000.00 to $15000.00, and his trade would have been equivalent to approximately $8500.00 at that time. I clearly remember in the early 1990s, when I was playing banjo for Doyle Lawson, we were at the IBMA awards show in Owensboro KY and my good friend Larry Perkins had 3 Original Fivestring Flatheads laying out on a bed in his hotel room. Two 3's and a 75 if I remember correctly! The thing I'm getting at is this..none of these banjos would have been priced higher than $18500.00! However, their price may

The inlay pattern is the standard catalog style 7 all the way, and this neck also features a handstop. Many of the style 75's that feature maple necks have no handstop whatsoever, and have a very narrow neck width. See "The last RB-75" featured in this book to view this type of RB-75 neck.

ONLY KNOWN ORIGINAL 5 STRING RB-75 WITH STYLE 7 INLAY AND PEGHEAD.

The Steve Huber RB-75 has a very comfortable sized, great playing neck, and also features a full uncut Mastertone label, 20 hole full weight flathead tonering, and came originally with Kluson amber button tuners with Phillips head screws. It also features Philips head screws in its L-brackets, and

PERFECT UNCUT LABEL.

PHILLIPS HEAD SCREWS IN L BRACKETS.

LATER STYLE LARGER KNURLED THUBSCREW.

as well have been $185,000.00, for few people, including myself, could even think of coming up with that much money for a banjo at that time.

This may sound extremely low when compared to the prices that these same banjos will command today, but one must remember, this was a lot of money 20 years ago. It is very close in line with what they are bringing today when 1989 dollar values are compared. The US dollar was much stronger then than it is today, and therefore had a lot more purchasing power. The value of the dollar has

FRICTION 5TH PEG, 5TH STRING NUT.

declined considerably since then, and its value at any given time is extremely important in any highly collectable market. In declining financial times almost certainly some Country will excel in buying power, and therefore buy up highly rare collectables such as art, antiques, and highly rare musical instruments. If a person studies the histories of different Countries and also their fluctuating wealth, they will see that these highly collectable markets change hands and sometimes Countries approximately every 25 years. This can be viewed by looking back at a very prosperous Japan of the 1980's, as they nearly bought up all the best examples of both electric and acoustic guitars, as well as many very nice examples of banjos and mandolins. Many of these same instruments are now back here in the States today.

A lot of wealth has filtered into the United States in the past decade with new upstart internet companies making millions of dollars very quickly. Some of this new found wealth was spent on Guitars, Banjos, and Mandolins, therefore driving prices and demand for them upward and very quickly.

This RB-75 is an extremely rare "one of a kind example", and I would like to thank Steve Huber again for allowing us to photograph it here in these pages.

SERIAL NUMBER STAMPED INTO BACK OF PEGHEAD.

Provenance:

1. Shipped from the Gibson factory, Jan. 30th 1940, to Walburg and Auge in Worchester Mass.
2. Purchased by its first owner Mr. Leon Warren, Feb. 3rd 1940, for $106.50.
3. Whereabouts unknown for several years until it shows up in a PA music store for sale. Circa. Mid 1980's
4. Purchased by its current owner Mr. Steve Huber. Circa. Mid 1980's

ORIGINAL 5 STRING TENSIONHOOP.

The Last RB-75?

The Last RB-75?

This banjo is a rare bird indeed, as it doesn't conform to any catalog model at all. It can only be described as what pre war Gibson banjo scholars have dubbed a "Floorsweep". This term was devised to try and help describe a very late 30's or 40's model production Gibson banjo that was put together when the Gibson factory was in very low supply of materials. Too low in fact to complete these particular banjo orders to the standard catalog model specs, and ended up using whatever parts were on hand and readily available to get an order out the door. This was a somewhat common practice right before and during WWII.

(See the J. D. Crowe RB-75 in this book for more facts outlining Gibson's Wartime situation)

Several types of materials commonly used by many different factories before the War were in short supply, especially highly useful military items such as brass and nickel were being heavily used and rationed for war use. The Gibson Company stayed alive by simply digging through their factory bins and clearing off dusty shelves to find and use older already manufactured parts in order to fill and complete the very few banjo orders that would have come in during these wartime years.

PEGHEAD WITH LARGE FLEUR DELIS, AND FAT SCRIPT GIBSON INLAY, ALSO LARGE BELL SHAPED TRUSSROD COVER WITH PHILLIPS SCREWS, ALSO FIRST INLAY IN FINGERBOARD TURNED SIDEWAYS.

All that stated.... I'll add that "Floorsweep" is also a term that's very loosely used, and I'll say again.. a term to be extremely cautious of when considering buying an expensive, supposedly all original, Pre War Gibson Flathead banjo, as many unscrupulous banjo "mechanics and butchers" have pieced together banjos using all original pre war Gibson parts, rims, necks and resonators that did not come from the factory at the same time at all, and then called it a "Floorsweep". Some of these banjos can be very convincing to the casual banjo enthusiast, and can also look "right" and even sound very good. As mentioned before, the pre war Gibson factory's unmistakable hand and original intent, can usually clearly be seen by the banjo scholar who's handled, owned, and studied enough of these highly rare examples to know the difference.

This banjo is what appears to be a true "Floorsweep" banjo and features no serial number or label, other than what appears to be a factory COD shipping label affixed to the inside of the rim with a date of 1-24-44. If this is indeed an actual ship date this banjo could certainly be considered one of the last if not "the last" RB-75 shipped out of the factory before the end of WWII.

This banjo features a full weight, high profile 20 hole nickel plated tonering, rock maple neck with a somewhat rare, but well known inlay pattern, and no handstop. The resonator is odd in that it doesn't conform to any other known standard model Gibson banjo. It is of highly figured maple with plain white binding. The grain of the maple in the resonator reminds one of a style 6, high grade of curly maple veneer. The finish on this banjo is quite thick and darker in color. I've seen several War-time Gibson guitars finished in this same color with this almost grainy finish job. It's not sloppy in its application, but does lack in that it maybe was not buffed and finished out to the same high degree as the finish on earlier produced instruments. The rim on this banjo could have originally been intended for a lower than Mastertone grade banjo, such as a style 1, as the dark brown color conforms to this, but it could have also been made for a style 7 top tension banjo. But this rim only has 3 resonator lugs, which could be explained by the factory assembler only being able to find three L brackets and thumbscrews rather than the standard 4. All Mastertone banjos normally featured 4 resonator lugs.

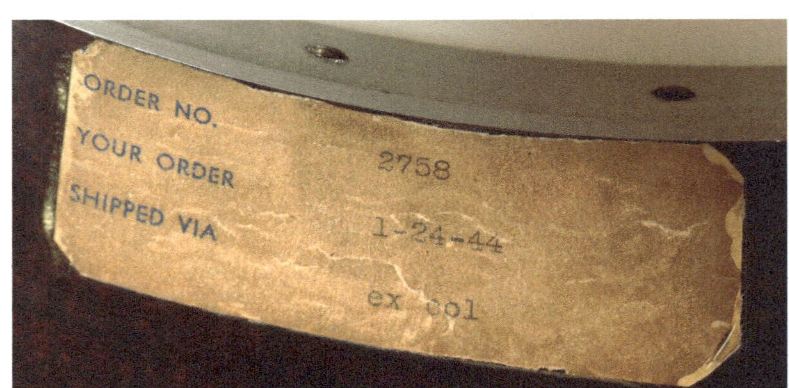

BELIEVED TO BE FACTORY ORDER SHIPPING LABEL.

The label inside this banjo is odd in itself, and I've never seen another like it. It states an **Order Number of 2758, your order of 1- 24-44,** and a **shipped via ex coll,** which is believed to mean it was shipped Jan. 24th 1944 with a COD (cash on delivery) payment required. The "coll" stood for collect.

BACK OF PEGHEAD SHOWING EARLIER 1920'S STYLE GROVER TUNERS, NO HANDSTOP, AND DARK BROWN WAR TIME FINISH ON STRAIGHT GRAINED MAPLE NECK.

The inlay pattern on this RB-75 banjo is rare but is well known on several other all original RB-75's. It's seen mainly on banjos with these very slim rock maple necks with no handstops. Curtis McPeake and I have discussed these rare necks at length several times, and have come to the conclusion that these necks were possibly made from existing RB-00 neck blanks. The RB-00 was the cheapest model RB- resonator 1 pc flanged banjo, and featured rock maple on most examples. These RB-00 neck blanks would have worked without a problem on these Mastertone pots, as both featured the one peice flange design. Another reason for thinking this is that all known examples feature fingerboard inlays that are turned sideways at the first fret. The reason for this is that these necks are so slim at the nut, that the first inlay won't fit if turned the normal way. Another fact is that all known examples with shipping records were shipped very late from 1941 forward. Another fact concerning these highly rare banjos is that they either don't feature a Mastertone block in the fingerboard at all, or only have a pearl block that's never had anything engraved on it. The examples without a block have the same 3 pearl dots as seen on this example, standard on the style

1 banjos inlay pattern of the day. These banjos also all feature the same strange peghead overlay. It seems that these overlays were originally intended to be used on 1930's and 40's Gibson Lapsteels, and feature the fat "Gibson" inlay in script of the time

period with a fleur delis in the center of the overlay. These clunky peghead overlays don't even fit the layout of a double cut banjo peghead design very well. As can be seen on this RB-75, the bottom of the "G" in the pearl "Gibson" on the peghead inlay actually runs underneath the third string tuners washer in every example of these banjos that I've seen.

This banjo also features a tenor tensionhoop which may or may not be original to this banjo, we don't know for sure.

I do know of a few original fivestring banjos that were shipped with tenor tensionhoops originally from the factory. This banjo also features the thicker fingerboard binding seen on all of these banjos and also on some of the later model top tensions.

It's a very rare banjo indeed and could be the last RB-75 known to ship out of the factory. I would like to thank my good friend Mr. Darrell McCumbers for allowing us to photograph it for this book.

Provenance:

1. Purchased by John Wheat from George Gruhn Dec. 5th 1987

2. Purchased by Andy Cartoun April 14th 1990

3. Acquired by Don Sojka in a trade with Andy Cartoun April 9th 1992

4. Purchased by current owner Darrell McCumbers circa. Late 1990's

ORIGINAL TENOR STYLE TENSIONHOOP, WITH NO MASTERTONE BLOCK.

The Hubert Loar RB-7

SERIAL NUMBER E2791-1

The Hubert Loar RB-7

This banjo shipped out of the Kalamazoo MI plant, January 16th 1942 to the Fred Walker Music Company. The next time this banjo would show up in history is when Mr. Hubert Loar acquired it secondhand sometime in the mid to late 1940's in Baltimore MD. We don't know for sure from whom or where in Baltimore it was purchased at this time, but Hubert Loar soon moved near Tyler Texas, and played many dances and contest with this banjo throughout his lifetime. The banjo descended to his son Earl Loar upon his death, who sold it to Brian Sims of Slaughter LA, who then sold it soon after to my good friend Dan Loftin of Nashville TN, who also just happened to take all the photographs in this book. Dan has long been a fan of the Toptension designed Pre War Gibson banjos and has owned several of them over the years. Dan kept this banjo for a while and then sold it to its current owner, Mike Mueller.

STANDARD STYLE 7 INLAY AND TENSIONHOOP.

The toptension style of Gibson Mastertone banjo was introduced in 1937, and was a total new departure from the standard old pot construction of the early and mid 1930's design of Gibson Mastertone banjo. This newer design included a remarkable new way of adjusting the head tension from the top side of the banjo without having to remove the resonator. Thus garnering them the name "Toptensions" in later years. This was a major selling factor the factory must have thought, for at this time the only banjo heads available were the calf skin type that would be in use until the late 1950's when mylar heads became available. These calf skin heads were very fickle in humid weather and therefore required constant adjustment if played regularly. The thicker and heavier tensionhoop and bracket construction, along with the new solid carved resonator, replacing the earlier plied veneer type were some of the major changes in the design of these new banjos. The newly designed armrest on these banjos also allowed a quicker removal with the simple adjustment of a single knurled thumbscrew. This in turn allowed full access to the 24 brackets on the top side of the banjo for head tension adjustment. These banjos were quite a bit heavier than the earlier standard design, and also featured a bigger bolder looking peghead shape which took advantage of the newly popular art deco fad sweeping the country at that time.

The banjo featured here doesn't conform to the typical standard catalog specifications of the model completely, but very few toptensions do. There were very few made to begin with, and we know that in the late 30's and early 40's prior to WWII, the Gibson factory had an extremely low inventory of banjo parts. They also weren't producing many new ones as there was a limitation order demanded by our Government decreasing all musical instrument output. The Gibson factory's war effort was the major reason many late examples of Gibson banjos feature odd or non standard parts, wood types, or plating's, that stray from the catalog descriptions. This being said... be careful in your search for one of these banjos, for this situation has created a problem for some unwary buyers, as unscrupulous people have pieced together a bunch of old banjos parts and called it a late 30's or early 40's Gibson "floor sweep model banjo, saying that.." you know they (the Gibson factory) were just throwing anything together they could at this time before WWII".

I am still however a firm believer that these 1930's and 40's Gibson factory workers original intension's, through their hand skilled labor can still be easily seen and verified today. They created a type of handwriting if you will, that true Pre War Gibson scholars can read very clearly, even in these banjos, however odd they may be. I will also add that this knowledge is not easily nor inexpensively gained, and requires much time and patience, and a very good memory of many previously seen examples that the person judging the banjo has had the opportunity to examine thoroughly. Very few have obtained the experience that enables them to be able to identify a really good "out and out fake" from an "absolutely 100% original, but slightly odd late example banjo" that may be totally different from catalog specs, but still fully factory original.

The first of the non standard features on this banjo would be the peghead inlay. Although this large fleur delis inlay is seen on several well known original examples of this model, it wasn't the standard catalog version. The style 7 pegheads generally had an inlay which more closely resembled the fingerboard inlay. It's kind of a "Bow Tie" inlay, with slashes cut into the side. See the Steve Huber RB-75 peghead for the correct style 7 inlay.

This RB-7 also features an oddity inside its rim. There's a piece of inlaid binding on the bottom edge of the rim, that's only seen on style 6 banjos fingerboards and resonators, known as "checkerboard binding". I know of a few other totally original banjos of different styles that feature this same oddity inside of their rim. We really have no idea why the factory would do such a thing but it's typically seen in very late examples such as this, shipping out of the factory in the very late 1930's or early 40's. The only thing that makes sense to me is that they were actually using up rims that may have been culled at some point for some sort of small defect in the rim, and installing this binding was a way of hiding this imperfection and making it into a useful sellable rim again.

This banjo also has an extremely "fiery" piece of curly maple in its neck. This is a very desirable trait in any maple banjo, and adds greatly to its overall appearance. It features the newly popular "Stair Step Kluson" tuners with amber buttons, which are quite rare, and only seen on later toptension models, and also on a few electric banjos that Gibson was producing at this same period. The serial number

STANDARD STYLE 7 PEGHEAD SHAPE, WITH NON STANDARD LARGE FLEUR DELIS, AND FAT GIBSON IN SCRIPT INLAY, ALSO LARGE BELL SHAPED TRUSSROD COVER WITH PHILLIPS HEAD SCREWS.

MASTERTONE LABEL RAN UP INTO TONERING, BUT I WOULD STILL CONSIDER THIS AS UNCUT.

is stamped into the back of this RB-7's peghead also. The rest of this banjo conforms to catalog standard with dark finished maple resonator and neck, nickel plated metal. The Mastertone label is basically full, with a fine 20 hole flathead tonering.

The style 7 banjos catalog description included all nickel plating, and they also featured a Grover nickel plated clamshell tailpiece, which this one still retains. These tailpieces are extremely hard to find today if they are lost or broken. It's much easier to find an original chrome or gold plated clamshell than a nickel plated one, simply because more models were made featuring the chrome and gold one. The style 7 is the only model Gibson banjo that I know of that featured a nickel plated Grover clamshell tailpiece. As stated Gibson used the gold clamshell on many high grade models, and the style 12 toptension of the same period featured a chrome plated Grover clamshell as did the earlier 1930's style 4 banjos. But these nickel plated versions are extremely hard to locate today.

This banjo otherwise conforms to catalog specs and is a fine example of an original fivestring RB-7. I would like to thank both Dan Loftin and Mike Mueller for allowing me to know about it, and also photograph it for this book.

PROVENANCE:

1. January 16th 1942 shipped to Fred Walker.
2. Hubert Loar purchased it used approx. 1945 Baltimore MD
3. Descended to his son Earl Loar
4. Purchased by Brian Sims 1999
5. Purchased by Dan Loftin 2000
6. Purchased by current owner Mike Mueller 2003

BACK OF PEGHEAD SHOWING THE MORE RARE LARGER KLUSON AMBER BUTTON "STAIR STEP" TUNERS, AND SERIAL NUMBER STAMPING.

The RB-12

SERIAL NUMBER 411-2

The RB-12

This RB-12 was brought to light by Mr. Ricky Wasson, who purchased it from the original owner's family in KY, where it had resided its whole existence. Music store owner and guitar great Ricky Wasson has also been the lead singer in J D Crowe's band for many years now. He purchased this banjo from its original owner's family, and then sold it to Melvin Cumbee of Chas. SC; he then traded it to Darrell McCumbers all in the same year. Isn't it amazing that a banjo that has remained in one place for so many years can then trade hands and travel through several different states in less than a year's time! This banjo had always appeared to be 100% original in every way to me, but it had the strangest serial number stamping on the inside of the rim that I'd ever seen. The die stamp that was used on this serial number inside the rim was totally different than any other banjo from this period that I'd ever documented. Even though this stamping was totally different from any other Pre War Gibson banjo I'd ever seen, I knew the rest of the banjo to be 100% original, because I not only knew every part of it to be original, but I knew where it came from.

THE RAREST FORM OF SERIAL NUMBER STAMP.

I also knew very well that there were 2 distinctly different die stampings used on serial numbers from the early 30's up into the early 40's. When the factory started stamping serial numbers in the back of the pegheads in the late 1930's they used a completely different type of die stamp than they had previously used to stamp the inside of the rims throughout the 20's and early 30's. They also began to incorporate letter prefixes into their serial numbers at this time. This 411-2 stamping really had me stumped though, as it was larger in overall height than either of the previous known two types, and also the numbers were very straight and very plain, unlike either of the other two afore mentioned types of stamping. They were still stamped inside of the rim also, so I concluded that they should be in the back of the peghead if they were stamped any later than 1938. I was almost to the point of talking myself into believing that this banjo had come from the factory without a serial number at all, which was not at all uncommon in the pre WWII, toptension years, and maybe the original owner or the next had "monkeyed" with this perfectly original specimen of an RB-12 himself, and made these stampings himself. This is one of those times where you know what you're looking at is totally "right", but you are seeing something totally new to you, so you have to rely on your stored knowledge of banjos in the past that you've seen and studied. A lot of people would have labeled this rare serial number stamp as having been "fooled with", but I'm glad I kept looking for answers.

That was until August of 2006, when I saw a banjo that Mandolin Brothers had previously sold that was a very rare prototype or experimental banjo if you will, with a 12 inch head. This banjo was an original 5 string, and the serial number was stamped inside the rim plain as day. These numbers were made from the exact same factory die stamp as the 411-2 serial numbers in this banjo! Elderly Instruments had another one of these experimental banjos, a tenor that has the same type of stamping, so the Gibson factory did in fact have 3 distinctly different stampings for serial numbers at the same approximate time. Since then, I've located another totally 100% original TB-7, belonging to my friend Craig Korth with this same serial number stamping. This is just another one of those never say nevers when you're dealing with something out of the ordinary on pre war Gibson banjos. When you think something looks right, but can't possibly be factory original, stop, think again, and do your research!

This RB-12 banjo is totally 100% catalog standard in every way and fully original. It's a wonderful example of a very rare banjo. It features a walnut resonator and neck, and a lightly shaded sunburst finish with chrome plated metal. It also has the Grover clamshell tailpiece and 20 hole flathead tonering and uncut Mastertone label, and still features its original friction 5th peg. This banjo features the two band Grover tuners also used on mid 1930's style 4 banjos. It seems they stuck with the standard 1930's style 4 appointments on the style 12 such as walnut wood, and chrome plating, and even the same tuners and tailpiece.

One after market feature that's seen on this banjo will be found on several toptensions. They are the small nuts on the bottom of the tension brackets inside the resonator. These were added because in their efforts to find a new way to tighten the heads from the top without taking the resonator off, Gibson neglected to think about the wear and tear of the threads inside the holes on the flanges which were made of simple pot metal. The constant tightening and loosening of the brackets to adjust the head tension many times resulted in stripped threads on some of these banjos, therefore the small nuts on the brackets takes care of this. This in no way harms the originality or integrity of the banjo, and doesn't affect its value to the collector or player one bit.

I would like to thank my good friend Darrell McCumbers for allowing me to photograph this extremely rare RB-12 for this book.

TOPTENSION PEGHEAD DESIGN, SHOWING FLATHEAD SCREWS IN TRUSSROD COVER, AND BOUND AND INLAID IN THE 12/18 STYLE.

PROVENANCE:

1. Original owners family in KY
2. Ricky Wasson purchased it circa 2001
3. Melvin Cumbee purchased it circa 2001
4. Traded to Darrell McCumbers circa 2001

PERFECT UNCUT MASTERTONE LABEL.

SIDE OF RESONATOR DISPLAYING STANDARD WHITE/BLACK/WHITE BINDING AND CHROME PLATED METAL.

FLATHEAD SCREWS IN L BRACKETS, RARE ORIGINAL ARMREST THUMBSCREW, AND ADDED NUTS ON FLANGE BRACKETS.

The RB-18

SERIAL NUMBER 744-1

The RB-18

This banjo shipped out of the factory December 2nd 1938 to C. B. Ellis Music Company in Burlington NC.

Nothing much is known of its history until the 1970's when a good friend of mine who wishes to remain anonymous purchased this fine example of an RB-18 circa. 1974. He has owned and enjoyed it for over 30 years now. He'd known about this banjo for a good while before purchasing it, but beyond that we don't have a lot of early history on it.

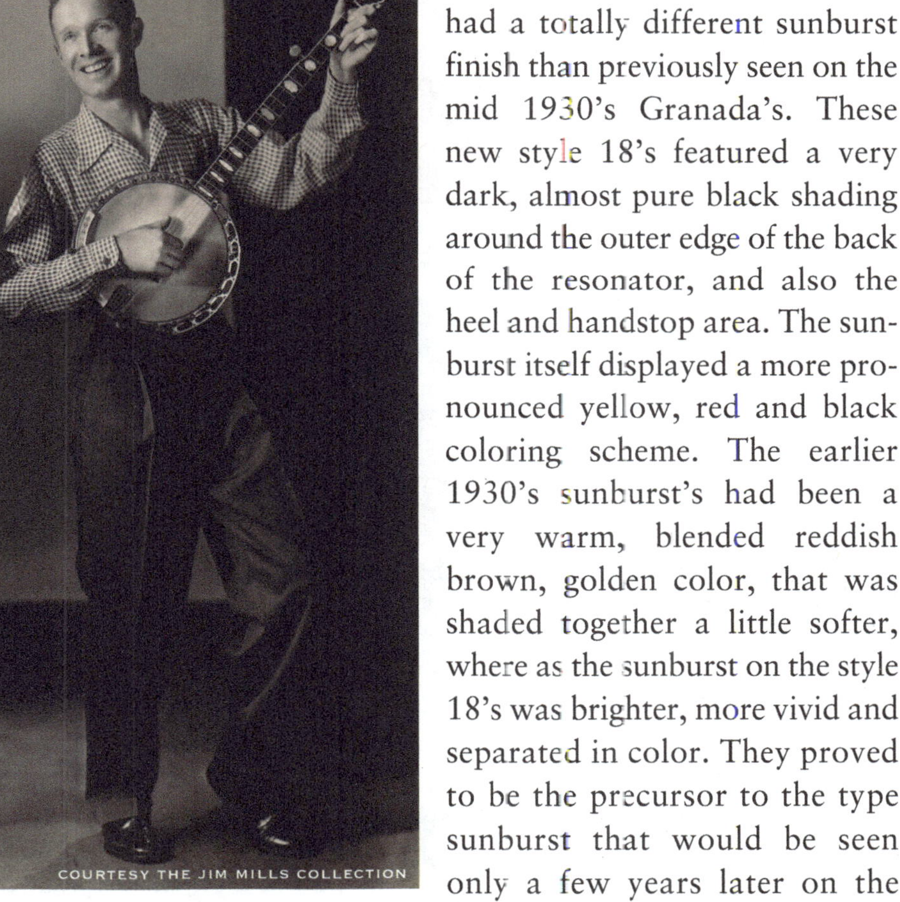

COURTESY THE JIM MILLS COLLECTION

Original RB-18's in general are an extremely rare lot, as I only know of less than half a dozen existing. This was the top of the line banjo after 1937 with the advent of the new Top Tension style, and sold for $220.00 brand new. The fivestring banjo was probably at an all time low at this time in America, and not many fivestrings of any type were selling, much less Gibson's top of the line, highest priced model. This had to have been one of the first RB-18's to be shipped out of the factory in late 1938, as they had just been introduced less than 24 months earlier.

These banjos were gold plated and very well engraved and usually featured very nice "curly maple", "blistered maple" or "birds eye maple" wood. This banjo features an exceptionally even grained very tight curly maple pattern on both its neck and resonator. Some style 18's are seen with a so called "blistered" maple grain, which is kind of a combination of curly and birds eye maple grains, and then some examples have all birds eye maple grain. They also had a totally different sunburst finish than previously seen on the mid 1930's Granada's. These new style 18's featured a very dark, almost pure black shading around the outer edge of the back of the resonator, and also the heel and handstop area. The sunburst itself displayed a more pronounced yellow, red and black coloring scheme. The earlier 1930's sunburst's had been a very warm, blended reddish brown, golden color, that was shaded together a little softer, where as the sunburst on the style 18's was brighter, more vivid and separated in color. They proved to be the precursor to the type sunburst that would be seen only a few years later on the first post war Gibson banjos..The style TB, PB, and RB-100's.

Scotty Wiseman of "Lulu Bell and Scotty" fame also had one of these rare original RB-18's, and is featured here in this original photo playing his RB-18 without the resonator, which he was very well known to do.

PERFECT UNCUT MASTERTONE LABEL.

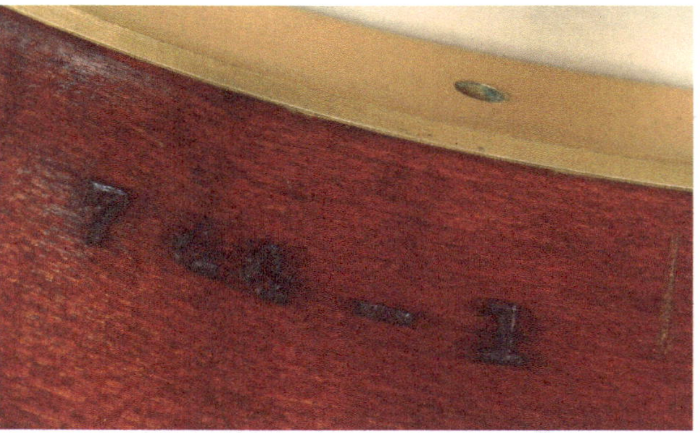

THREE DIGIT SERIAL NUMBER STAMPED INSIDE RIM WITH NO "PAT. APPLIED FOR"

STYLE 18 ENGRAVING , PHILLIPS HEAD SCREWS IN L BRACKET, AND NEW ADDED NUTS ON SOME BRACKETS

WHITE/BLACK/WHITE BINDING AND RARE ORIGINAL KNURLED ARMREST SCREW.

Back to this RB-18 serial number 744-1, this banjo features a perfect uncut Mastertone label, and serial number stamped inside. This RB-18 was made right before Gibson began stamping the serial numbers into the back of the pegheads. This banjos serial number was still stamped with the standard old die stamp used throughout the mid 1930's, and not the odd larger plainer die stamp seen on the RB-12, Sn 411-2, also featured in this book. This odd stamp is still a mystery and is only seen on a very few banjos before they started being stamped behind the peghead.

These style 18 banjos are certainly a beautiful combination of curly maple, engraving, and gold plating, and as I said they are extremely rare, with less than 6 original RB fivestrings known to exist.

This particular RB-18 banjo for some unknown reason seems to have had a nickel plated armrest. It appears to be totally original in engraving and plating, and the only explanations I can come up with are that it was gold plated over nickel and the gold has been completely worn off, or was cleaned, and left this way, or it was made of steel rather than brass, and therefore would look like this when the gold plating got worn off, or it was simply never gold plated to begin with, and shipped out nickel plated.

The owner for the past 35 years says he purchased the banjo exactly like it appears right now, and that the armrest looks the same as it did then. Two different plating's seen on the same banjo are certainly nothing out of the ordinary during this period of banjo production.

Style 18's either came with the Grover two band tuners or the later bigger square shaped "Stair Step" Kluson tuners, seen on RB-7, Sn 2791-1 featured in this book. This RB-18 also retains its original large amber Catlin tuner buttons which are very rare. They were only used on the highest grade of Mastertone banjos such as style 6's, Granada, 18's, Bella Voce, Florentine, and All American. Most of these high grade banjos generally featured solid Mother of Pearl tuning buttons, but occasionally they used these Catlin buttons. Catlin was a very popular new material with the 1930's deco generation, and was used to make all sorts of decorative items such as ashtrays, lamps, jewelry, and just about any type of small factory produced item of the era.

Both the style 18 and style 12 Top Tension banjos featured the same newly designed, art deco inspired, octagonal motif inlay pattern in the fingerboard, and an almost two dimensional skyscraper looking inlay, with a diamond shape in the center of the peghead. This banjo also features the "Fat Gibson" pearl inlay in the peghead. This was a new departure from the finer cut "Gibson" seen in earlier 1930's models. Both this fatter and the finer cut "Gibson" were used at the same time on top tensions and also RB-75's up until production ceased with the start of WWII.

This RB-18 features a finely shaped neck and is a true pleasure to play. It's also one of the finest sounding Top Tensions I've ever played. I would like to thank my old friend for allowing us to photograph it for use in this book.

PEGHEAD SHOWING THE STANDARD STYLE 18 SHAPE AND INLAY, ALSO THE LARGE SIZE BELL SHAPED TRUSSROD COVER AND PHILLIPS SCREWS.

PROVENANCE:

1. Shipped out of the Gibson factory December 2nd 1938 to C. B. Ellis Music Company, in Burlington NC

2. Sold to unknown original owner. Circa 1939

3. Sold to another unknown NC native circa. 1970

4. Sold to my friend and current owner, who wishes to remain anonymous in 1974.

ORIGINAL SLIGHTLY ARCHED FINGERBOARD WHICH WAS STANDARD ON ALL TOPTENSIONS

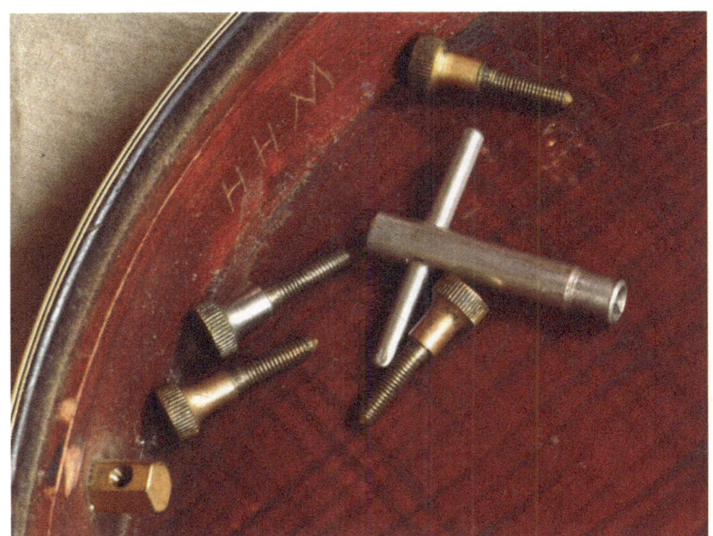

INSIDE RESONATOR SHOWING INITIALS H.H.M., AND THE SOLID, NOT PLIED CURLY MAPLE BACK WOOD, ALSO FOUR SMALL KNURL THUMBSCREWS, AND VERY RARE ORIGINAL TOPTENSION WRENCH.

REGULAR OR 5 STRING BANJOS

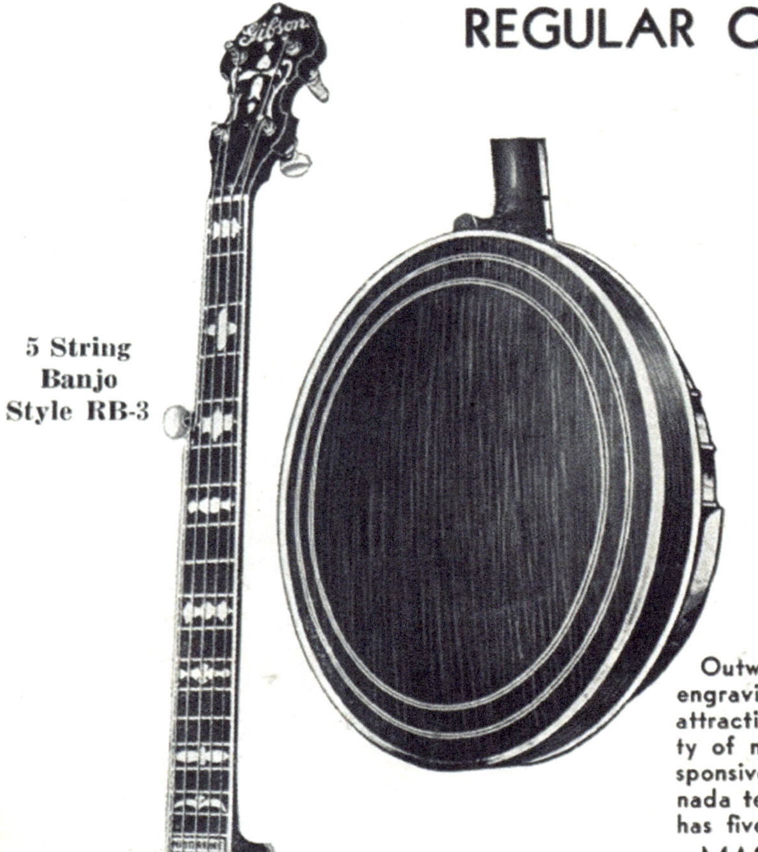

THE five string banjo is often called the "original American instrument" — improved and modernized by Gibson—same construction and scale length as Gibson plectrum banjo except has the extra fifth string starting at fifth fret. Tuned D B G C G.

MASTERTONE STYLE RB-GRANADA

$200.00

CASES
No. 521 Faultless $13.50
No. 522 Faultless 22.00

Outward beauty of gold plating, engraving, burl walnut woods and attractive decorations—inward beauty of matchless tone, power and responsiveness—same as style TB-Granada tenor banjo on page 33, except has five strings, 27" scale and 22 frets.

MASTERTONE STYLE RB-4

$150.00

CASES
No. 521 Faultless $13.50
No. 522 Faultless 22.00

Beautiful burl walnut and chromium plating—see style TB-4 tenor banjo on page 35 for description but with regular five string banjo neck, 27" scale and 22 frets.

MASTERTONE STYLE RB-3

(Illustrated)

$115.00

CASES
No. 521 Faultless $13.50
No. 522 Faultless 22.00

See description of tenor banjo style TB-3 on page 36, just the same except for 27" scale, five string fingerboard, 22 frets and has special rim construction.

STYLE RB-00

$27.50

CASE: No. 121 Challenge $5.00

Similar to style TB-00 tenor banjo on page 39 except has regular five string fingerboard with 27" scale and 22 frets.

STYLE RB-11 **$60.00**

CASE: No. 521 Faultless $13.50

The flashiest five string banjo made—same construction and special pearloid decorations and colors as style TB-11 tenor banjo on page 39—has 27" scale and 22 frets, regular 5 string fingerboard.

— 42 —

PAGE FROM THE 1934 GIBSON CATALOG. NOTE HYBRID BANJO IN PHOTO ENGRAVING HAVING A 2 PC. FLANGE AND DOUBLE CUT PEGHEAD. THESE PHOTOS CAN BE CONFUSING TO SAY THE LEAST.

An Economic History of the Gibson Pre War Flathead Fivestring Mastertone Banjo

It seems almost unimaginable to most Pre War Gibson banjo enthusiasts today, but this particular type of Gibson banjo was not very well received at all when it first became available. In fact if judged on unit sales alone, the original fivestring flathead Mastertone would surely be considered a complete and total flop. There were very few old-time, rural 5 string banjo players, who could even imagine being able to afford one of these new highly priced five stringed Mastertone models. Many of these banjos were ordered and purchased new by upper class banjoists of the day. These would have been mostly classical players, and only a few of them would have been interested in this newer styled Gibson resonator banjo anyway, as the more popular high grade Vega's, S. S. Stewarts, and Fairbank's, were still considered tops in the classical banjo world. Some of these Gibson banjos were purchased new by pre bluegrass, old time players. The majority of these guys seem to have been rural southern folk, who also would have certainly been the minority, having a stable job in these harsh economical times. I know of one such instance where a NC gentleman was employed by the Railroad, with a good paying job during the depression, who was able to purchase an RB-Granada in 1934. I know of another RB-Granada, ordered and purchased new in 1933, by a WVA gentleman who was a very successful prohibition era moonshiner.

These are but two stories of the few rural old time players able to afford such an extravagance as a flathead fivestring Mastertone banjo in the early post depression days. You have to remember the Tenor banjo was still King, and most of the rural old time 5 string players still played the smaller, open back form of banjos. This type of banjo could be purchased for only a few dollars at this time. The least expensive Gibson Mastertone was the style RB-3 banjo which sold for $115.00 at that time brand new. This was considered a great deal of money in that era. Most of the flathead fivestring Mastertone banjos that ended up in the hands of old time 5 string players were generally purchased second hand, in pawnshops, or from their original owners, who found they needed the extra money more than the banjo a few years later. It would be nearly 15 years after their inception before a young man from North Carolina would show the true potential of the Gibson flathead fivestring Mastertone. In December of 1945, Bill Monroe hired a 21 year old Earl Scruggs, who would prove to be the greatest influence the five string banjo playing world would ever know. Mr. Scruggs had been hearing, and playing this newer three finger style in his home state of NC for several years. He'd been influenced by other early North Carolina banjoists, but mainly by a relative named Smith Hammett, his older brother Junie, and local radio star DeWitt 'Snuffy" Jenkins. Earl and his new banjo sound were very well received immediately, and in a big way. He was being featured regularly by his employer Bill Monroe, on the strongest radio broadcast of the time, to feature string band music, later to be called "Bluegrass".

The station was WSM's "Grand Ole Opry", broadcast from the old Ryman Auditorium in Nashville TN. Although this style of banjo playing had been well known to many in both North, and South Carolina, since the mid 1930's, mainly through the picking of Snuffy Jenkins, and a few others on radio, this was a relatively small group of people listening to the broadcast of only a few local radio stations in their area. These early broadcast on stations like WBT in Charlotte NC, and WIS in Columbia SC, reached the Carolina's on up into Virginia, and Tennessee, but that was about it, whereas the far reaching signal of WSM, in Nashville TN, with its 50,000 watt clear channel was huge, and could be picked up across a large portion of the entire country. In the 1940's, there were several bands incorporating what we now know as the standard Bluegrass instrumentation, but the music that Bill Monroe's band would develop and record in just 2 short years of 1946 and 47, featuring Earl Scruggs, was far tighter and more rehearsed than anything preceding it. Although they only recorded 28 sides, their catalog absolutely set the standard for everything we know today as "Bluegrass Music". From fast and furious instrumental breakdowns, to slower duet ballads, to tight harmonies on their gospel quartets, they had it all. This band would influence more musicians, and these recordings would make a larger impact overall than any other string band known before them.

BILL MONROE AND HIS BLUEGRASS BOY'S CIRCA 1946. NOTICE EARL IS STILL PLAYING THE NON MASTERTONE, 30'S RB-11.

This legendary band consisted of Bill Monroe on vocals, and mandolin, Lester Flatt on vocals, and guitar, Earl Scruggs on vocals, and banjo, Chubby Wise on fiddle, and Howard Watts on bass, and vocals. From old radio transcripts of the Grand Ole Opry recorded live in 1946 and 47, we can hear this band nearly bringing the house down, with thunderous applause at the old Ryman Auditorium. A large part of this applause was no doubt due to Earl Scruggs nearly stealing the show each time he would take an instrumental break on the banjo. Opry announcer and innovator George D. Hay began introducing Earl as "Earl Scruggs and his Fancy Banjo"! Soon there were banjo players all over the country trying to emulate what they were hearing Earl Scruggs play on Saturday nights at the Opry. They were also beginning to take notice of just what type of banjo he was playing at his many live performances with this band.

I would venture to say that this is the beginning of these banjos starting to receive any sort of special notice outside of the Carolinas, where they were already highly revered. This was because many of the native North Carolinian pioneers of the 3 fingered style were already using Gibson banjos exclusively by the 1930's. In the mid 1940's, most any of these banjos could easily be purchased when found, for quite a bit less than they had sold for originally, less than 10 years earlier. No one was actively searching them out yet. We are talking in the neighborhood of a hundred dollars or less for most any of them even in the late 1940's. The first documented prices, and histories of any of these banjos selling, after their new retail prices, are the Snuffy Jenkins transactions, starting with RB-Granada Sn. 9584-3. Snuffy purchased this banjo directly from Fisher Hendley, its original owner, around 1936, for an undisclosed amount, believed to be less than $150.00, because we know he sold it less than five years later to Don Reno for $90.00. Snuffys personal favorite banjo however was RB-4, Sn. 9639-1. Snuffy found this banjo in a Spartanburg SC pawnshop in 1940, and paid $40.00 for it. This banjo had sold brand new only a few years earlier for $175.00, including its deluxe plush lined case, and factory original headguard. This only bolsters the fact of how hard times really were in rural America, and plainly shows the buying power of the post depression dollar in the rural South. I guess in essence this would make Snuffy Jenkins the first dealer/trader of pre war flathead fivestring Gibson Mastertone banjos in the Pre Bluegrass world.

RARE PHOTO OF DON RENO AND EARL SCRUGGS ONSTAGE TOGETHER AT "NEW RIVER RANCH" IN RISING SUN, MD. CIRCA 1957.

.

The popularity of these particular banjos in NC, SC, VA, and TN was no accident, and no doubt largely due to Mr. Dewitt "Snuffy" Jenkins early usage of them on radio broadcast, in performance, and recording with them also in the early 1930's. I also believe that's why a big portion of them seem to have migrated to this part of the country, and are still sometimes found there today. These are the four main States where radio broadcast by Snuffy, could be heard playing the newly popular 3 finger style, as early as 1934, on a pre war Gibson banjo. Snuffy is noted as being the first to perform the new 3 finger style on any radio broadcast, and also one of the first to use metal fingerpicks exclusively to be heard on radio and to stand out. I personally believe that both Reno and Scruggs were heavily influenced by Snuffy Jenkins in their early years as to what kind of banjo was best to play this newer 3 finger style on and also their use of metal picks. Both of these boys were listening to him on the radio, and also coming to see him perform live in their area. Snuffy was nearly 20 years older than either of them, and they surely must have looked up to him in some way. I also find it hard to believe they wouldn't have noticed what kind of banjo he was playing, a "big, shiny, and very loud, Gibson Mastertone", with a bunch of pearl inlay all over the neck. What I'm getting at is this... I don't believe these two young boys viewed Snuffy Jenkins the same as any friend of the family, or relative who just happened to play the banjo occasionally, but as a professional musician on stage, making a living at something other than farming. As mentioned earlier, most of the banjos these young boys were accustomed to seeing their local 5 string players playing were the simple open backed type of instruments. Look at any of the photos of the earliest known proponents of the 3 fingered style such as Smith Hammett, or Rex Brooks, or any of the other influences they may mention, and you'll see these men playing this same type of simple little open backed banjo. Earl Scruggs has told me personally that it seemed that he just grew up knowing that a Gibson Mastertone was "the banjo" to have, and I truly believe that this seed was largely sown early in his life, consciously or subconsciously by Snuffy Jenkins, and later came to fruition with both Reno and Scruggs finding their own Flathead Fivestring Mastertones to play throughout their careers! Both Scruggs and Reno came into contact with Snuffy Jenkins early in their lives, and both would also start their professional careers working on local radio stations in North and South Carolina. This not only greatly increased the popularity of the three fingered style in this small region, but also helped to make this particular type of Gibson Mastertone banjo even more popular here, earlier than anywhere else in the country. Of the 19 Original Flathead Fivestring Mastertones featured in this book, 11 were originally located in NC, SC, VA, and TN. There were also other influences playing these particular banjos in the 1930's and 40's on radio broadcast and at live shows throughout the Carolinas, such as Wade Mainer, Johnny Whisnant, Hoke Jenkins, Clay Everhart, Mack Crow, and also the afore mentioned Fisher Hendley. We have to remember that even though these banjos were relatively new at this time, they were still not easy to locate even in this part of the country where they were the most sought after. Although you the reader may think you've already read about a whole bevy of different original flathead fivestring Mastertone banjos, let's review here... we've really only discussed three banjos being sold here! Snuffy had already found and purchased both the RB-Granada, serial number 9584-3, and the RB-4 serial number 9639-1 by the year 1940. Don Reno bought the Granada directly from Snuffy in 1940, and around 1947, while still working for Bill Monroe, Earl Scruggs found a fine 1938 RB-75 serial number 518-1 in VA. He played this banjo for a short while, recorded briefly with it, and traded it to Don Reno for the earlier mentioned RB-Granada. These 3 banjo sales are really the earliest documented transactions of any 1930's designed,

COURTESY THE JIM MILLS COLLECTION

FISHER HENDLEY WITH HIS BAND "THE ARISTOCRATIC PIGS" PLAYING 1930'S FLYING EAGLE INLAID GRANADA. CIRCA 1938.

one piece flange, pre war Gibson flathead fivestring banjo, known to sell into the hands of musicians playing our type of music, Bluegrass. These three men, and these three banjos, I believe are the true nucleus of why any of these banjos are now collectable, and are totally responsible for the Flathead Fivestring Gibson banjo phenomenon that we enjoy today.

The late 1930's and 40's definitely brought about the first generation of North Carolina based Flathead Fivestring Gibson Mastertone players in the newer 3 fingered style. A few of the earliest pioneers would have to include Johnny Whisnant playing a late 30's RB- 75, with a full Flying Eagle inlay pattern, whereabouts now unknown, Mack Crow playing the only known Gold plated, standard inlay RB-75, Clay Everhart playing a 1930's RB-Granada with Hearts and Flower inlay, Hoke Jenkins playing the only known 1930's RB-6, Rudy Lyle playing a 1930's Wreath pattern RB-3, and the most influential player before Earl Scruggs hit the scene would have to have been Mr. Dewitt "Snuffy" Jenkins playing both a 1930's RB-Granada with Hearts and Flowers inlay, and also a 1930's RB-4 with Flying Eagle inlay . A few other fellows featured on radio broadcast, and recordings, who were very influential at this time, were Wade Mainer playing his 1930's RB-Granada with a combination Hearts and Flowers- Flying Eagle inlay pattern, and Fisher Hendley playing two different 1930's RB- Granada's, one with Hearts and Flowers, and the other with Flying Eagle inlay. Both of these men played in a combination 2 and 3 fingered style. Four of the nine of these historical banjos mentioned here are featured in this very book, and every last one of these pioneering gentlemen hailed from the Great State of North Carolina.

From the mid 1940's post WWII era we move to the music of the early 1950's. This was an explosive time for this new style of music later to be called "Bluegrass". Several different bands were emerging following the lead of the earlier Monroe Band, featuring Scruggs on banjo. These bands were writing and recording their own material, and much of their output is now considered "The Golden Era of Bluegrass". This would include the newly formed Flatt and Scruggs band, The Stanley Bros., The Lonesome Pine Fiddlers, featuring Ray Goins on banjo, Hylo Brown and the Timberliners, featuring Jim Smoke on banjo, Reno and Smiley, Jimmy Martin and the Sunny Mountain Boys, featuring J. D. Crowe, The Osborne Bros., and Jim and Jesse featuring their first banjo player, Hoke Jenkins. All of the banjo players in each of these bands, with the exception of Ralph Stanley, personally sought out an original pre war flathead Gibson Mastertone banjo to record and perform with. Ralph created his own distinctive sound by playing an archtop banjo, and therefore had an identity early on in his career, because he sounded so different from the majority of the other players. It's almost impossible to fathom today but by the mid 1950's, nearly every Major Record Label in this country had its own Bluegrass act signed to an exclusive recording contract. Columbia had Flatt and Scruggs, Mercury had the Stanley Brothers, RCA had both the Osborne Bros.and The Lonesome Pine Fiddlers, Starday had Hylo Brown, King had Reno and Smiley, Dot Records had Mac Wiseman, Jim and Jessie signed with Capitol, and of course Decca Records had both Jimmy Martin and Bill Monroe.

At this time, most of these original flathead fivestring banjos could still be purchased at relatively low prices when found, as no one had really thought much about them being collectable, after all, many of them made in the mid 30's were still less than 20 years old, and simply considered another plain old Gibson banjo. This would be equivalent to a mid 1980's instrument today.

I believe the main reason that allowed folks to view these banjos in a slightly more collectable sense, was the extreme rarity of them, even at that time. If you had the money, knew exactly what you wanted, and could afford one, these banjos were still extremely difficult to find, and purchase. This holds true today. It's been estimated that in basically the twelve year period, give or take a year, that these banjos were manufactured, (1930- 1942) less than 200 of these Original Five string Flathead, one pieced flange, Mastertone banjos were ever made. That figure is almost laughable today when you consider the amount of new banjos the Gibson factory and other companies can churn out in just a few months time. If the totals were added up to include a year's production of new reissue Gibson RB-3's, Granada's, JD Crowe RB-75 models, and all the different Earl Scruggs models mfg'd today, it would absolutely eclipse the entire production (over a decade) of the pre war 1930's designed 5 string Mastertones. So you can see how extremely rare these particular pre war Gibson banjos are, when compared to today's standards of manufacture.

COURTESY THE JIM MILLS COLLECTION

EARL SCRUGGS PLAYING HIS 1930'S RB-11. CIRCA 1946.

Let me clarify one thing, there were literally thousands of Pre War Gibson Mastertone banjos manufactured, predominantly the tenor or TB, and most were of the archtop tone ring configuration, but we are only discussing original 1930's and early 40's, factory produced, Original Five String Flathead Mastertone banjos in this book, and not any other type of Gibson banjo. Not even the now extremely desirable and valuable four string tenor, and plectrum original flathead banjos from this same period, as no one was converting these to fivestring at this time. Note.. even though there is a 2 piece flange designed, RB-6, featured in this book, this is an extremely rare one of a kind banjo, and because of the period of its manufacture it rightly deserves a place here, but 99.9% of these banjos were of the 1930's, one piece flange design. I personally believe that the estimated figure of 240 of these banjos being manufactured is too high, and I don't think anywhere near that amount were ever produced and therefore can't exist today. I have actively searched for these banjos all over the world for 20 years now, as well as comparing notes with other colleagues concerning their total known, factory original flathead fivestrings, and I know of approximately 115 existing that can be fully verified as original. I've owned 9 of them, currently own 5 of them, and have been fortunate enough to have played over 65 of them. I am however fully convinced that there will be several more previously unknown examples that will turn up, in say the next 15 to 20 years. I would estimate perhaps 40, but not 140, Original Flathead 5 string Gibson Mastertone banjos, that have been previously completely unknown to the entire pre war Gibson banjo community for more than 70 years now. All that stated, let's look at how long it took several of the pioneers to find their own Flathead Mastertone banjos even in the 1940's when they weren't collectable at all, and only a few years old. Snuffy Jenkins played a simple Gibson RB-1, with no tonering for several years, before purchasing the RB-Granada from his friend and co worker Fisher Hendley in the late 30's. Earl Scruggs was working regularly on the world famous "Grand Ole Opry", traveling all over the country with the most successful band of his time, Bill Monroe and the Bluegrass Boy's, making $60.00 a week, a very good salary in 1946, yet he played and recorded with a simple 1930's Gibson RB-11, with no tonering for nearly 2 years before finding the RB-75 Mastertone that he would later trade to Don Reno. Earl would have had the best opportunity in the world, traveling with this band, to see nearly every original flathead fivestring Mastertone banjo available in the whole Southeastern part of the United States. And please take into account that at this time most of these banjos were less than 10 years old! So you can see how rare they were even then. Reno pretty much had it easy from the beginning, because he was fortunate enough to purchase his first flathead fivestring directly from his mentor Snuffy Jenkins, while still in his teens, and didn't have to go looking for one.

COURTESY THE JIM MILLS COLLECTION

DON RENO AND EARL SCRUGGS CIRCA MID 1950'S.

I still find it incredibly hard to believe that it all comes back to one man, Snuffy Jenkins, playing that 3 fingered roll back in 1936 on that one banjo, RB-Granada Sn. 9584-3. It was owned, played, bought, sold, and traded by the 3 most important pioneers, and influential men ever to play in the 3 fingered style. Snuffy Jenkins, Don Reno, and lastly Mr. Earl Scruggs where it found a permanent home. That's still so incredibly ironic to me!

If the 1930's and 40's are considered the first generation of the North Carolina based 3 fingered style, flathead Gibson Mastertone players, then the 1950's and 60's are surely the second generation. The 3 fingered style, and the overall respect for this particular model Gibson banjo had by this time spread all over the country. Some of the Luminaries that came to prominence during this period are, J D Crowe, Sonny Osborne, Joe Medford, Hoke Jenkins, Oren Jenkins, Billy Edwards, Jim Smoak, Bud Brewster, Bill Emerson, Donnie Bryant, Porter Church, Jo Drumwright, Bud Rose, and Curtis McPeake. Most of these men had searched out and found their own original flathead Mastertone banjos by the mid to late 1950's. This was the first wave of any type, of an all out search for these banjos. Up until this time, all of the pioneers of the 3 finger style had found their own original Flatheads within a few years, but these younger fellows coming along in the early and mid 50's, mainly influenced by Scruggs, and Reno wanted a banjo just like their hero's, or at least as close as they could get. These fellows will plainly tell you that it sure wasn't as easy as deciding you wanted one of these banjos, and just going out and buying it. As I said earlier, even then these banjos were very hard to come by, and highly respected. I've thoroughly researched the history and prices realized on several banjos that I currently own or have owned in the past that were sold during this time. These prices were either quoted to me by the actual persons who paid them, or their immediate family members, and I have no reason to doubt them whatsoever. Some of the earliest documented prices that I know of being paid for these banjos after the pioneers of the three finger style began playing them are the Posie Roach RB-75, selling secondhand for $100.00 in Sept 1941. It was only a year old at the time. The next is the Bill Worrell RB-75, selling in 1947 for $100.00 from the original owner. This was ten years after it had been purchased new, selling for probably very close to its original retail price. The first record setting price that I know of, that really opened people's eyes, was the sale of a banjo I know very well, for I've owned and played it for many years. It's the Mack Crow Gold RB-75. Mr. Mack Crow was one of a handful of players considered a true pioneer of the three fingered style of NC, and was mentioned by Earl Scruggs in his landmark instructional book as an influence back in 1968. Mr. Crow ordered a gold plated Mastertone banjo from the factory around first of the year 1940, and got a highly customized Gold plated RB-75 in June of 1940. Mr. Crow kept this unique banjo for 12 years, and sold it to Mr. Avery Aiken of Statesville NC, for **$500.00** in 1952, a nearly unheard of sum for any banjo to bring in those days. This was a full 2 years before the first Post War Gibson Mastertone banjo would appear, later dubbed the "Bowtie" RB-250 in 1954. They were priced at $275.00 in the 1955 Gibson catalog featured here. This $500.00 sale was almost twice the cost of the new RB-250. This is really the first documented proof that I have showing that banjo players were beginning to realize that these old pre war Gibson flatheads were undoubtedly superior, and therefore more desirable, and more valuable than any new banjo for the Bluegrass style of music. I've spoken with several old timers that

MODEL NUMBER	ITEM	LIST PRICE INCL. FED. EXCISE TAX
	5-STRING BANJOS	
RB-100	5-string Banjo	$165.00
RB-150	5-string Banjo	225.00
RB-250	Mastertone 5-String Banjo	275.00
121	Challenge Case for above models	12.75
521	Faultless Case (Flannel) for above	39.00
522	Faultless Case (Plush) for above	43.50
	PLECTRUM BANJOS Available on special order; write for prices.	
	UKULELE & TENOR UKULELE	
Uke-1	Ukulele	$ 27.50
30	Chip Board Case for above model	3.25
TU-1	Tenor Ukulele	42.50
111	Challenge Case for above model	6.00
	FINGERREST PICKUPS The following units will be attached to Guitar selected. See description of L7-CE (L7C with No. 102 pickup) in electric circular.	
100-SN	Single, Nickel (L-7, S-300)	$ 37.00
101-SG	Single, Gold (L-5, L-12, S-400)	39.50
102-SCN	Single, Cutaway, Nickel (L-7C)	37.00
103-SCG	Single, Cutaway, Gold (L-5C, L-12C, S-400C)	39.50
104-DN	Double, Nickel (L-7, S-300)	63.50
105-DG	Double, Gold (L-5, L-12, S-400)	66.00
106-DCN	Double, Cutaway, Nickel (L-7C)	68.50
107-DCG	Double, Cutaway, Gold (L-5C, L-12C, S-400C)	70.00
	ZIPPER COVERS	
ZC-5	Zipper Cover for 514 and 515 cases	$ 23.00
ZC-6	Zipper Cover for 606 and 600 cases	25.00
ZC-4	Zipper Cover for 300 and 400 cases	30.00
ZCG	Zipper Cover for 13 case	15.00
ZC-LP	Zipper Cover for 535 Les Paul Guitar Case	21.50
ZC-CLP	Zipper Cover for 537 Les Paul Custom Case	21.50

Prices subject to change without notice and all orders are subject to prices in force when shipment is made.

Tenor Guitars and 4-String Plectrum Guitars available in some non-cutaway models on special order—$25.00 extra.
Write for prices and delivery dates on cutaway and left-handed models.

ZONE 1

Effective September 15, 1955. All prices subject to change without notice. To improve the design, quality, and performance of our units and to make use of the best available materials at all times, we reserve the right to change specifications without notice.

1955 GIBSON PRICELIST

COURTESY THE JIM MILLS COLLECTION

knew Mr. Crow personally, and remembered this banjo being for sale, and they relayed to me that it seemed like he had it for sale a pretty good while. One older gentleman from that area told me, "yeah I remember it very well, every banjo picker in that whole damn country down there wanted that banjo, but nobody could come up with $500.00!, that is until Avery Aiken came in from Statesville and bought it". This demonstrates just how tight times were in the rural south. This part of the South was hard hit by the depression, as farming was the main vocation, and for many folks the effects of the depression didn't end over night. My own dad was born in 1933, and remembered very well, as a small child, going to town on Saturday afternoons in the late 1930's and early 40's and seeing as many horse drawn buggy's and wagons as there were cars, parked on the streets of his Southeastern VA hometown. Now that's Hoover town! He said several of these folks had automobiles but couldn't afford to buy gas to put in them, and were mainly doing business on the barter system by trading goods for other goods. This only led to more rural folks holding onto their dollars a little harder and longer even up into the early 1950's until good jobs became more available and more people began to prosper. To add a little perspective to the value of the US Dollar, and just how much $500.00 was worth at this time in America, my Grandfather purchased a small farm in Southeast VA in 1948 for $1750.00! The next banjo sale I have documented in price, was Mike Longworth's trade of a Gibson parts banjo with a trade in value of $300.00 for an original flathead fivestring RB-4 from Earl Scruggs in 1958. Earl had priced this RB-4 flathead at $600.00 outright. I would think that Earl more than likely had his finger on the pulse of the market as close as anyone, as to how much these old banjos would actually bring, and I would venture to say that this was more than likely the going rate for most any good old flathead fivestring at this time. That is when sold by anyone who knew what they had. However there were still many of them bought for much less than this, from original owners who had paid around $100.00 for them new, and were happy to make anywhere from $20.00 to $50.00 dollars profit on, "just another old banjo" in their eyes.

PHOTO: PHIL ZIMMERMAN

SONNY OSBORNE PLAYING HIS FULL FLYING EAGLE PATTERN RB-75. CIRCA 1976.

Sonny Osborne told me the story of how he paid $250.00 for his Full Flying Eagle pattern, circa 1937 RB-75 in 1956, from a Dayton OH Music store. This was very much in line with the price of the new model RB-250 banjos being produced at this time, but was still a good deal. Up until then he had been playing a very good 1920's style 3 Gibson archtop 5 string,, the only original pre war Gibson fivestring that he could find at the time, but he already knew what he really wanted, an original flathead fivestring Mastertone! J. D. Crowe told me of how he traded a 1950's RB-100 for his first flathead style 3 in an even swap, because his RB-100, a banjo he only kept as a backup, had a good skin head on it, and was immediately playable. The owner of the style 3 didn't want to fool with the labor and expense involved in changing the busted calfskin head on his style 3 banjo, so he swapped him even for the RB-100. Curtis McPeake said in an earlier interview in BU that even in the early 1950's, amongst the better banjo players, it was already pretty much common knowledge that the older Flathead Mastertone's were "the only type of banjo to have". He also told me the story of how he bought his old RB-75, affectionately known as "Ole Betsy", for $100.00 in 1958. This was an extremely good deal even at that time.

COURTESY THE JIM MILLS COLLECTION

J.D. CROWE CIRCA 1970'S.

As many of the newly formed Bluegrass bands began to record, and perform live, all of these banjos we've just mentioned could be seen and heard at live shows, and also heard regularly on the radio. Not long after this, many of the remaining old Original Flathead five stringed Mastertone banjos were sought out, and bought up by the few players who were fortunate enough to know what they were looking for, and then find them. A lot of these guys seeking a five string banjo were young men who had went to War in the 40's listening to, and liking Country music, and had now come home just in time to hear this exciting new type of music, with soaring vocal harmonies, screaming fiddles, and blistering banjo solos. They had never heard anything like this, and they loved it. They too wanted to try and emulate what they were hearing Earl Scruggs and others do on the radio, jukebox, and records just a few years later. Also most of these folks now had good steady jobs, thanks to the post WWII job boom, with plenty of work to be had. After a few years of prosperous saving from a good job they also had a little extra money to spend on something like an expensive Mastertone banjo for the first time in their lives. The problem was there were no new Flathead Mastertone Gibson banjos being produced at the end of WWII, only simple RB-100's with no tonerings at all and simple dot inlays. The Gibson Company had surely been taking notice of this newer craze in acoustic music, with more folks requesting 5 string resonator banjos in particular than any time in the past 20 years. They proceeded to build their first Post War Mastertone around 1954, and designated it the RB-250, now known to collectors simply as the "Bowtie" because of its inlay pattern, which resembles a bow-tie. These banjos were first introduced with an archtop tonering, and later changed to the flathead type of ring around 1957. I'm not sure what prompted them to change to the flathead design but they sure switched in a hurry, and began producing flatheads only in the Mastertone line. As the supply of the old original pre war 5 string Mastertones was quickly depleted, the Gibson Company capitalized greatly on this, for their 1950's, and 60's Bowtie Mastertone banjos sold well. They were good enough banjos, but their overall quality and construction lacked much, when compared to the banjos produced throughout the pre war years. As early as the mid to late 50's, a few serious students of banjo tone began listening more closely to the pioneers of the Pre War Flathead banjo sound, guys like Earl, Don, Sonny, and J D.. They realized that these guys were getting a different tone than most everyone else, and they began studying just what type of banjo these guys were playing. Joe Drumwright, Bud Rose, Curtis McPeake, Bud Brewster, Mike Longworth, Paul Champion, Tom Morgan, Rual Yarborough, Pete Kuykendall, and early vintage instrument dealer Harry West, were some of the earliest to recognize this.

Earl Scruggs being a very sharp business man, also noticed the demand for these older pre war Gibson banjos, and began trading in them from time to time. Earl undoubtedly encountered more of these banjos than the average fellow would, while traveling the road, and playing over such a long period. Many owners of these banjos would simply bring them out to a Flatt and Scruggs performance, just to show them to Earl. I know the same thing happened with Reno and Smiley from my own personal experience of searching and trading in these banjos for over a 20 year period now. I can honestly tell you that at some point in the past 50 years, either Earl Scruggs or Don Reno had already seen, played, owned, or tried to buy, nearly every original flathead fivestring Mastertone that I've been able to uncover in my lifetime. It seems that I have been "cold tracking" these guys and these banjos all of my adult life! If you doubt this, read the inside cover of the old Red and White covered, 1959 Flatt and Scruggs "Picture Album, Hymn and Songbook". In his "Suggestions for banjo beginners", Earl Scruggs placed a small advertisement in the bottom right corner to "those who might be buying new Gibson instruments" at the bottom of the ad he relates that... "I occasionally have one or two of the old Mastertones for sale".

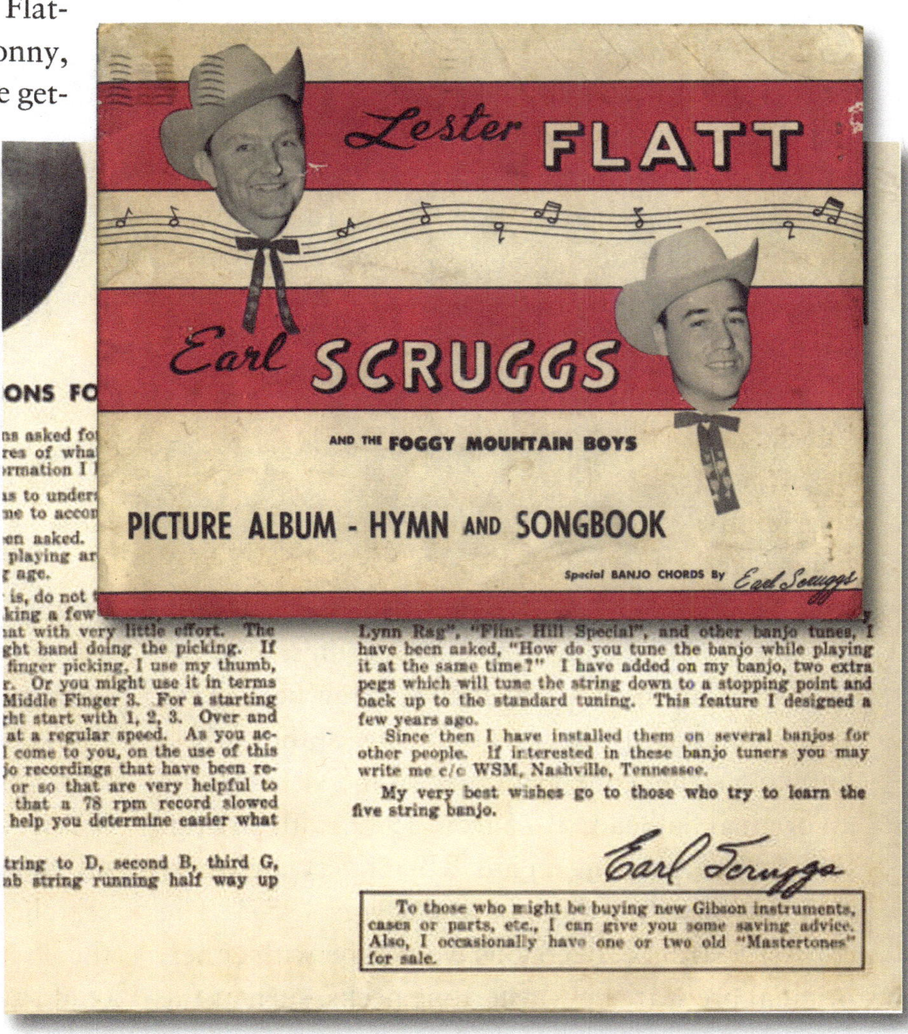

ONS FO

...at with very little effort. The ...ght hand doing the picking. If ...finger picking, I use my thumb, ...r. Or you might use it in terms ...Middle Finger 3. For a starting ...ght start with 1, 2, 3. Over and ...at a regular speed. As you ac... ...l come to you, on the use of this ...jo recordings that have been re... ...or so that are very helpful to ...that a 78 rpm record slowed ...help you determine easier what

...tring to D, second B, third G, ...mb string running half way up

Lynn Rag", "Flint Hill Special", and other banjo tunes, I have been asked, "How do you tune the banjo while playing it at the same time?" I have added on my banjo, two extra pegs which will tune the string down to a stopping point and back up to the standard tuning. This feature I designed a few years ago.

Since then I have installed them on several banjos for other people. If interested in these banjo tuners you may write me c/o WSM, Nashville, Tennessee.

My very best wishes go to those who try to learn the five string banjo.

Earl Scruggs

To those who might be buying new Gibson instruments, cases or parts, etc., I can give you some saving advice. Also, I occasionally have one or two old "Mastertones" for sale.

Earl also mentioned when discussing the "Old Model Mastertones", on page 149 of his landmark instructional book "Earl Scruggs and the Fivestring Banjo" in 1968, that "these banjos would be considered a bargain today at prices from $500.00 to $1000.00". This gives us some real factual insight as to the true worth of these banjos at this time. I have a 1961 Gibson catalog that advertises the new RB-250 Mastertone 5 string at a price of $345.00. This is definitely proof that these pre war Flathead Gibson banjos were already considered far superior, and steadily increasing in price even at this early time.

This is when the original flathead five string Mastertones definitely came into their own and became known as "The only Banjo to have". It's also the start of when a few sharp luthiers and collectors began to realize that the more plentiful, tenor and plectrum original flathead banjos, and also their archtop cousins could be converted into 5 strings, with the simple addition of a newer five string neck. I recently purchased what has to be one of the earliest known 5 string conversion banjos in existence. It's an original flathead PB-75 from 1939, with an original 1930's batwing inlaid RB-1 fivestring neck, that was fitted to this pot as early as 1957! The earliest 5 string conversions were done with either, original pre war sub Mastertone necks, such as the

"FRETS" MAGAZINE COVER FROM FEB. 1985 FEATURING SEVERAL ARTICLES ON "VINTAGE INSTRUMENTS."

original fivestring RB- 1 necked banjo that I just mentioned, or the simple 1930's RB- 00's dot inlayed 5 string necks. Another option was the newer 1950's RB-100, 150, or RB-250 Bowtie Mastertone necks which were easy enough to fit to pre war tenor or plectrum pots. This was just the beginning of a phenomenon that today, over 50 years later, makes it very hard to locate any completely unmolested tenor or plectrum Gibson banjo from this period. As the supply of the extremely rare Original Flathead Fivestrings were far too few to meet demands, these banjos quickly became nearly impossible to locate after the 1960's. The rush on any type of pre war Gibson banjo soon followed, and Gibson's archtops were the most commonly found. Also the more rare original flathead tenors and plectrums began to be more highly revered because they were the next best thing to owning an original fivestring flathead. The earliest known 5 string conversions of these tenors and plectrums, with completely newly built fivestring necks known to me, were made by Tom Morgan, Robby Robinson, Bob White, Walt Pittman, J W Gower, Randy Wood, and Marion Kirk. This newfound interest in all types of pre war Gibson banjos only fueled the search, and interest, in the most rare and elusive, the "Original Flathead Five String" when they could still be found. This also created a noted increase in the prices of these extremely rare banjos when one would rarely show up for sale.

In the late 1960's and early 70's several magazines dedicated to stringed instruments and Acoustic music began to pop up, such as Mugwumps, Pick' in, Bluegrass Unlimited, and later Frets, which featured articles and specific columns related to vintage stringed instruments. Many of the top collectors, dealers, builders, and repairmen, of the day, such as Harry West, Tom Morgan, George Gruhn, Stan Jay, Randy Wood, and Tut Taylor began placing ads and writing articles in these publications documenting these extremely rare Banjos, as well as Pre war Martin Guitars, and Gibson Lloyd Loar era F-5 style Mandolins. They printed serial number list that for the first time allowed owners and collectors to accurately date these instruments. They also reprinted many of the old original catalogs that had never been seen by most of the public at this time. For the first time they could see the catalog descriptions of the many different models of banjos that the Gibson Co. had manufactured throughout the years. This greatly increased the knowledge of folks recently introduced to Bluegrass Music, and created a newfound interest in all types of vintage stringed instruments, especially these old Gibson Mastertone banjos.

"BLUEGRASS UNLIMITED" COVER FROM NOVEMBER 1967 FEATURING SNUFFY JENKINS.

This is when many of the most dedicated banjo enthusiasts really began educating themselves concerning these old pre war Gibson banjos, reading and gleaning all they could from these articles, and discussing them amongst themselves. Also during the summer months, hundreds of Bluegrass and Old Time Music Festivals were cropping up all across America, and occasionally an old timer would drag out an Original Flathead Fivestring Mastertone, or Original Herringbone Martin D-28, or Loar F-5 mandolin that had not been in circulation or seen in many years, and conversations were of high interest concerning all of these rare instruments there also. This whole era did much to further the interest, and increase the knowledge in this highly collectable market of banjos, mandolins, and guitars.

One of the first establishments to specialize in buying and selling vintage stringed instruments, was GTR opening in 1970 in Downtown Nashville, by George Gruhn, along with partners Randy Wood, and Tut Taylor. George went out on his own a few years later as simply "Gruhn Guitars", and has become the Premiere Vintage Instrument dealer in the world today. George is extremely knowledgeable concerning most all vintage stringed instruments, and has bought, sold, and traded many original flathead Gibson banjos in the past 35 years. As a matter of fact, I would have to give him more credit than any single person, for steadfastly educating and promoting these rare instruments for nearly 40 years now, and also allowing the entire Vintage Stringed Instrument Community to thrive, and maintain the well informed place, that we all enjoy today. Through his writing of so many articles, in publications too numerous to mention here, and also his many authoritative books, he has made the public aware of the true qualities and value of American Vintage Stringed Instruments for over 35 years now. He has also placed more of these instruments in the hands of gifted players and serious collectors throughout the world than anyone else I can think of.

Another extremely knowledgeable and most important person concerning the authentication of these particular Gibson Mastertone banjos, who has also probably owned, played, bought and sold more original flathead fivestring banjos than any one person in the world is Mr. Curtis McPeake. He has owned and operated McPeake's Unique Instruments since 1975 in Mt Juliet TN, and is also a great banjo player. Both of these gentlemen are regarded the world over as two of the most knowledgeable scholars in these instruments, and I'm very thankful to call them both my personal friends. Mandolin Brothers of Staten Island NY opened their doors about this same time, and has been managed by Stan Jay to great success, specializing in vintage instruments also. Elderly instruments are another in Lansing MI, owned and operated by Stan Werbin. Harry West is probably the earliest collector/dealer of all these guys, and continues to trade at Harry and Jeanie West Fine Musical Instruments now located in Statesville NC. Harry realized early on the superior qualities of vintage instruments and began collecting in the 1940's. All of these dealers have done, and continue to do a fine service to folks

Classified Ads

BLUEGRASS UNLIMITED WILL ACCEPT CLASSIFIED ADS AT THE RATE OF $.20 PER WORD. All ads must be paid **IN ADVANCE** and received by the **10th** of the month prior to publication . So that your count will agree with ours, we count as one word, any grouping of letters or numbers.

ORIGINAL GIBSON: TB-6, late 20's, $1800.00. Fancy Washburn (Lyon & Healy) tenor banjo $500.00. Epiphone N.Y. deluxe guitar acoustic $450.00. Gallagher G-50, 12 string guitar $275.00. Pimental classic $350.00. Mark Swolsky, 4106 Jamesway Dr., Toledo, Ohio 43606.

GIBSON A-40: $200.00; Epiphone EB-98, $225.00 h/c. 301-722-5905.

BLUEGRASS COLLECTION FOR SALE: LP's & 45's, many collector items. For list write, Charles Williams, 299 Nash Road, Knoxville, Tenn. 37914.

BANJO FOR SALE: 1975 Gibson RB-800 Mastertone, Flying Eagle pattern, Viceroy brown finish. Mint condition and excellent quality. $1200.00 firm. Chuck Gordon c/o Taylor's Guitar Shop, Elizabeth, TN 615-543-3581.

BANJO PARTS AND ACCESSORIES: Send $.50 for the Steward-MacDonald catalogue of banjo hardware and do-it-yourself banjo kits. Steward-MacDonald Mfg., Box 900, Athens, Ohio 45701.

FOR SALE: 1941 D-28. Good condition $1500. Bob Brook 208-263-7247.

IMPERIAL HANDCRAFTED BANJOS: are available in five models, carry a lifetime guarantee, are priced competitive and produce an excellent sound. If you are not hung up on a name and just interested in the highest quality available please write, Imperial Banjo, 2527 SW 59th, Okla. City, OK 73119.

ORIGINAL GOLD ENGRAVED 1927 GRANADA MASTERTONE TENOR: HSC, $1050.00. 1952 F-12 Gibson mandolin, HSC, $650.00. Other banjos, violins. 219-456-9336.

FOR SALE: 1928 TB-5 Gibson Mastertone 40-hole, archtop, Gold plated, engraved, excellent condition. Bob Givens custom 5-string neck, $2000.00. Paramount style C 5-string original $1000.00. Tubaphone tenor $250.00. #7 Whyte Ladie plectrum $1000.00. Bacon Super banjo plectrum $300.00. Bob Heacox, 2607 Bridgeport Way, Tacoma, Washington 98466.

GIBSON ARCH-TOP #6:and Vega Whyte Ladie, both with original pots and excellent reproduction 5-string necks. Box 327 D, Rt. #4, Chestertown, Maryland 21620. 301-778-1380. Fully guaranteed repairs to all bluegrass instruments.

LIQUIDATING COLLECTION: 2 herringbones, 6 Gibson banjos. Send SASE for list. Fred Severud, 94 Maple Ave., Rockawav. NJ 07866.

IMPERIAL HANDCRAFTED BANJOS: are available in five models, carry a lifetime guarantee, are priced competitive and produce an excellent sound. If you are not hung up on a name and just interested in the highest quality available please write, Imperial Banjo, 2527 SW 59th, Okla. City, OK 73119.

GIBSON MASTERTONE RB-3:Original 5-string flat head wreath inlays, double-cut headstock, very rare, $4000.00. Late 30's Dobro, Square neck, 12 frets, 2 screen holes, excellent guitar, $550.00. Sunflower Music, 632 Portage, South Bend Indiana 46616. 219-288-5485.

CUSTOM MADE BANJOS: Tone rings and shells by Bill Gibson. Repairs and refretting. RD2, Reinholds, PA Phone 215-484-4266.

SACRIFICE: Upright Kay bass, good condition, with case. Bella Voce banjo, all engraved and gold plated, pre-war tone ring, hard shell case. 405-622-2660.

WANTED: Experienced young mandolin player to join group in Northern Virginia area. Must sing. Call: John Davis 703-860-2137.

JUST RELEASED! STI-105 - HOW TO PLAY CARTER-STYLE GUITAR: 13 tunes & songs the way Maybelle plays them, plus booklet with words, chords, tuning charts covering beginning to advanced techniques. Wildwood Flower, Lula Walls, Alabama Gals and ten others. Also: STI-101, Country Fiddle, Vol. 1; STI-102, Country Fiddle Vol. 2; STI-104 Clawhammer Banjo. Each $4.95 now, $5.95 after March 1st. Catalog $.25 from Sonyatone Records, Dept. B, PO Box 567, Santa Barbara, Ca. 93102

ARE YOU READY TO BUILD YOUR OWN BANJO AND DO IT RIGHT? If so, get our heavy ¾ maple rim with lathe fitted Buck Super Flathead tone ring, and new Gibson 1 piece flange. Just $159.50 complete. We guarantee this pot assembly to produce a super fine bluegrass sound. Tone ring is manufactured to old prewar specifications. This assembly may also be used to up-grade older RB 250's. If you don't need the new 1 piece flange, deduct $32.50. We offer a complete line of parts for banjos. Illustrated catalogue $1.00. First Quality Banjo, 5303 Galaxie Dr., Louisville, KY 40258. 502-447-5670.

30 TO 50% DISCOUNT: Dobros, Martins, Gibsons, others. Books, parts, records! Free Catalog! Warehouse, B-36, Box 11449, Fort Worth, Texas 76109.

HANDMADE ACOUSTIC GUITARS: James C. Boyce, Box 608-b, North Falmouth, Massachusetts 02556. Also guitar strings made to my specifications, reasonable prices. Write for details.

DOBROS: Best prices anywhere in the U.S. Color catalog $.40. Holiday Steel guitars, Winchester, IN 47394.

QUALITY DULCIMERS, PSALTERIES: Mt. style fretless banjos, thumb pianos. Buy as kits too. HERE, Inc., #B, 410 Cedar Ave., Minneapolis, Minn. 55404.

NEW BLUEGRASS/OLD TIME MUSIC RECORD COMPANY: Looking for dealers to handle albums we produce & distribute. Looking for individuals desiring a catalog of records. Over 325 titles of bluegrass, Texas fiddle, blues & ragtime guitar. Write: Ridge Runner Music, 3035 Townsend, Dept. BU-300, Ft. Worth, TX 76110.

5-STRING BANJOS: New OME, Gibson, Baldwin and others. New genuine Gibson F-5 mandolins. Lynn's String Shop, 104 N. Pennsylvania, Roswell, N. Mex. 88201. Phone: 505-622-0556.

NGM TONE RINGS: Will upgrade your tone and volume from 25 to 50% on any wood rim constructed banjo that takes 11" heads. We recommend our arch top ring when you have conversion in mind. If you doubt your own ability, Bill Blaylock will personally do your conversion and set up. Cost approximately $25.00, plus tone ring and any other new parts you wish installed. (Approximately two weeks service.) Write for free info on our rings. Builder-Dealer inquires invited. North Georgia Music Co., 2751 Canton Road, Marietta, Georgia 30062.

PRICES ON PRE-WAR GIBSON BANJOS AND PRE WAR MARTIN GUITARS FROM DEC. 1975 BLUEGRASS UNLIMITED CLASSIFIEDS.

searching for the right vintage stringed instrument for over 35 years now. One of the latest guys to enter the Pre War Gibson Banjo market, who's made a very big impact especially in the Original Flathead Mastertone world, is my friend and colleague Mr. Steve Huber. He began simply as a player, and connoisseur of these fine banjos. His background as a machinist and mechanical engineer naturally developed into him wanting to try his hand at making a tonering. He began making some of the finest replica flathead tonerings available, and this in turn developed into building his own line of banjos around these fine tonerings. Huber Banjos currently builds some of the finest banjos in the world today. I'm proud to play the "Huber Jim Mills Model", which is nearly an exact replica of my old "Mack Crow RB-75", featured in this book. All Huber banjos are meticulously crafted in every respect.

And lastly, not to plug my own business to much, but Jim Mills Banjo specializes in the sale, trade, and brokerage of nothing but Original Pre War Gibson Banjos. You can call me at 919 608 0355 or email me at jimmillsbanjo@msn.com

In regard to understanding the rapidly rising prices of these banjos in the past decade, I hope to help explain part of it through this. The main reason in my opinion is...before the advent of the internet, email, and Ebay, it may have taken a few years for prices on some items to have changed very much. This was simply due to the amount of time it may have taken for the news of an exact price of a recent sale to travel across the country, allowing other dealers and sellers to know the exact price a similar instrument had previously sold for six months or a year before, one dealer to another. Now with the internet, and email, these sale prices are known almost immediately. This in turn has allowed dealers to keep up with exactly what the market will bear at any given time, and after nearly every sale of a highly desirable rare item, when the next one of its kind becomes available for purchase it generally tops the price of the last one sold. Therefore prices have skyrocketed in just a very short while, on many types of vintage instruments, and other collectables. Also the internet in general has educated the entire country on just about anything you can think of. If you can pull it up online, in just a matter of seconds you can pretty closely determine its value, or at least find a website to further your quest. The days of finding the old farmer who still has his Original Flathead

"PICKIN" MAGAZINE FEATURING THE OSBORNE BROTHERS, OCT. 1979

Fivestring Mastertone banjo that he bought new in 1938, or an older fellow who has no idea of the worth of his daddy's old banjo are almost certainly a thing of the past today.

The fact is that the supply has simply never came close to meeting the demand for these particular five string flathead banjos for the past 50 years now.

Such quickly gleaned knowledge, worldwide, mainly due to the internet, has allowed the prices to rise steadily for the past 10 years, causing some of the rarest models to quadruple in price, in a mere 10 years.

In a November 1973 issue of "Esquire" magazine there is an article entitled "The return of the banjo", Snuffy Jenkins is quoted as saying he recently turned down an offer of $2000.00 for his Flathead RB-4 Sn 9639-1, featured in this book. I would say that he made a wise decision, because the next two record setting prices I have documented were only a few years away in 1977 and 78 with real landmark sales of two fine banjos. The first was the Butch Robbins RB-4 serial number 9583-1 featured in this book, which sold late in the year of 1977. Butch paid the first real record setting price of $6000.00 for this banjo, which was absolutely staggering at this time in America. Butch was working in Bill Monroe's Bluegrass Boys, the number one Bluegrass band in the nation, and wanted the absolute best banjo he could find and afford. This banjo was absolutely 100% original in every way, and almost like new from what I understand. Butch made monthly payments on it for five years, like a car or house payment. The next shocking sale was the RB-Granada serial number 9584-2 from Tom McKinney to Sonny Osborne, also featured in this book. This sale is almost singlehandedly responsible for raising the bar overnight on all pre war flathead banjo prices to a level that most thought they would never reach. When on New Year's Day 1978, Sonny Osborne paid $5000.00 for this Original Flathead Fivestring Granada, featured in this book; it shocked the whole banjo community. It was the talk of the town for quite a while, and Sonny was sure to let everyone know, probably more than any single person, just how rare these particular banjos were at the time. He told me personally that after he'd really stopped to think about "just how much money he had spent" on a banjo, it began to sink in. From Sonny's publicly educating folks by talking to them, personally showing them how great these banjos actually were, he felt he was merely protecting his investment! At this time in America a brand new High Performance Chevy Camaro or Ford Mustang could be bought for less than this. No one could believe any banjo could bring that much money. This opened the eyes of many, to the extreme rarity of these wonderful banjos, and also helped to show just how rare and in demand they actually were. To show just how little information was available on these banjos at this time, neither Tom nor Sonny even knew that

COURTESY THE JIM MILLS COLLECTION

BILL KEITH PLAYING STYLE 12 TOPTENSION CONVERSION, CIRCA 1960'S.

this banjo was the consecutively serial numbered mate to Earl Scruggs Granada! No one really knew much at all about serial number identification or anything like that at this early time. These two banjo sales seemed to secure the original flathead fivestring Mastertone banjos place in history, as a highly collectable, highly desirable commodity in the eyes of players, collectors, and just anyone interested in these old banjos, and made them stop and take another long look at them.

First of all, these particular banjos were so rare that, years may have gone by, before one would even come on the market offered for sale. This of course created a feeding frenzy when one did become available for purchase, and sometimes a bidding war erupted amongst potential buyers. These two sales in 1977 and 78 absolutely broke all records, raised the bar, and set a new standard for prices to increase rapidly in these rarest of Gibson Mastertone banjos for the next 20 years or more. In the 1980's Bela Fleck purchased an original flathead style 75 pot from Mandolin Brothers. Even though this banjo was not an original fivestring, it was still a huge shot in the arm for the original flathead Mastertones. And even though Bela was not known as the most traditional Scruggs style player, which are who were typically associated with these banjos, he chose a flathead 75 as his personal favorite, and it remains so to this day. This was nothing new though, for Bill Keith had paved the way for nearly all melodic/avant garde players in the early 1960's while playing on an original flathead, top tension style 12 banjo with Bill Monroe's Bluegrass Boy's.

COURTESY THE JIM MILLS COLLECTION

ACTUAL BANJO WORKSHOP IN GIBSON FACTORY, KALAMAZOO, MI. CIRCA 1920'S-30'S

Throughout the late 1980's and early 90's these original Flathead fivestring Mastertones, as well as their 4 stringed original flathead siblings continued to rise rapidly in price well into 5 figures, and now in the 21st century, several Original Flathead Fivestrings have sold in the six figures, and a few even rarer higher grade gold plated Granada's are reported to have brought over $200,000.

These banjos can finally, after over 75 years of existence, be likened to the best of Americana, or fine art if you will. They have reached a place in the world where their value is reflected by more than just their utilitarian worth as a superior musical instrument to play. They are regarded as the absolute best of their type ever produced. A benchmark that has never been equaled, much less bettered for the past 75 years. Don't get me wrong, I'm not of an attitude that they should all be put under glass in a museum, and only viewed by the public, never to be played again. I truly believe they should be played and recorded, but I also think they are on par with some of the greatest musical instruments ever made, and should be treated as such. They don't command the prices of Stradivari violins, but they are certainly considered the Stradivari of 5 string banjos in Bluegrass Music! They're also just as rare, and in as much demand in their own circles. Old Master Italian violins, and modern Classical music have got 250 years of existence on these banjos, and Bluegrass music in general for that matter! Remember, they only made an infinite number of these banjos, and they can only become fewer with each passing decade. When you account for loss in the US and abroad, by War, fire, flood, earthquakes, and other types of catastrophes throughout the years, a sizable amount have already been lost forever, possibly 10 to 15% of total production. Who knows what was lost across the entire Gulf Coast with Hurricane Katrina just a few years ago. Not to downplay the terrible loss of life in any way, but they say an untold amount of priceless art in the form of paintings, furniture, sculpture, and architecture was destroyed forever in that one day.

MY DAD, "JOHN WESLEY MILLS." I WAS 15 YEARS OLD IN THIS PHOTO. WHATEVER I MAY ACCOMPLISH IN THIS LIFE, I OWE THE MOST TO MY OLD "DADDY." HE WAS MY BIGGEST FAN.

Another thing I would like to address here are the grumblings I've encountered from many Bluegrass musicians over the years, concerning the rapidly rising prices of these extremely rare instruments. They've cried for the past 30 years "that the poor musician is the one who suffers most from these price increases, because the best instruments such as Original flathead Mastertone Banjos, Lloyd Loar era Gibson F-5 mandolins, and the highly desirable 1930's, and 40's D size Martin guitars are now only available to a very few players, and are being purchased mainly by wealthy collectors, and amateurs". Well I'm here to tell you that if you truly want one of these instruments bad enough, you'll find a way to acquire it. Butch Robbins found a way in 1977. Everyone said he was crazy for paying that kind of money for a banjo, but I would say he made a fine investment in his career as a professional musician and in life in general. As I said before he made monthly payments on it, like buying a new car.

You can take this advice for what it's worth to you.... I can honestly say, that in the past 25 years of watching these instruments closely, that I have never heard one single person, who invested in any high quality vintage stringed instrument say that they ever regretted buying it, and most have made a very handsome return on their investment when they decided to sell. The only people I hear complaining are the ones who are still waiting for the deal of a lifetime to suddenly fall into their lap, like an original Flathead Mastertone at a yard sale for $150.00, or for Aunt Ruthie to die and leave them a Loar F-5 Mandolin, or Pre War D-45 in their Will. The rest can continually be heard crying about "that 1937 Martin D-28 that they could have bought back in 1974, for $2500.00, and now they want $95,000.00 for one".

I ask that you take these few cold hard facts into consideration.....there are literally millions of Art Collectors all over the world, who own countless, very expensive old master paintings. They continually buy, sell, and trade them to upgrade their collections, but not all of them can own a Picasso, Renoir, or Monet. It's simply not feasible because of the law of supply and demand. In the Antiques World, Authentic American Chippendale furniture from the 18th century is some of the most highly prized in existence, but even the most avid antique collector may never get to own such a piece.

There are literally "millions" of classical musicians in both large and small Symphonies, and Quartettes, performing all over the world, many on very fine authentic 17th and 18th Century Italian Violin family instruments, but not all of them can own a genuine Stradivari, or Guarneri instrument.

Likewise there are tens of thousands of Bluegrass Musicians all over the world, but not all of them can have an Original Flathead Mastertone banjo, Lloyd Loar F-5 mandolin, or 1930's Martin Dreadnought guitar . There has never been enough of any of these instruments to go around, never! Not even 10 years after their manufacture!! If they were that easy to procure, they would not be collectable at all. One of the world's most renowned Flathead Fivestring Mastertone banjo collectors, scholars, and authorities, Mr. Curtis McPeake, summed it up perfectly in a recent article in Bluegrass Unlimited magazine when he said, "There was a time in America when any of these old banjos could be bought for less than $500.00, the problem was.. nobody had $500.00." So you see nothing has really changed all that much.

Some folks might say.. " yeah.. but that was a long time ago, what about today". Well, I'm very happy to be able to name some of the more modern professional banjo players of today, who've also found a way to procure their own original flathead Mastertone banjo. Just a few are.. Dana Cupp, Charlie Cushman, Mike Snider, Bela Fleck, Allison Brown, Scott Vestal, Craig Smith, Tony Trishka, Larry Perkins, Steve Huber, Sammy Shelor, Mike Scott, Dave Talbot, Kirsten Scott Benson, Bill Evans, Craig Korth, Mike Munford, Rob McCoury, Noam Pikelny and yours truly. So you see, they are still obtainable if you put things into perspective.

If you plan to be a Doctor, you need to try to get the best Medical education available to you. If you aspire to be a Lawyer, find the best Law school you can, and if you're Goal in Life is to be a Professional Musician, seek the absolute best instrument obtainable, in order to progress in all aspects of your type of music, and to help create all that you're capable of.

The supply and demand issue, and rapid price increases are really nothing new concerning any type of highly rare, collectable commodity.

I hope this short documentary on the economic history of these banjos is as interesting to others as it is to me, and good luck in finding one of these fine old banjos to play and enjoy for yourself.

Sincerely, Jim Mills

2008

Major Cosmetic Differences between early to mid 1930's Mastertones, when compared to late 1930's and early 40's style 75's and Toptension Banjos.

EARLY TO MID 1930'S MASTERTONES

1. More consistent overall, in finish color, inlay patterns, and all standard catalog features.
2. Only one dot at the 12th fret binding usually.
3. Thinner clear coat of nitrocellulose, that wears off very easily.
4. Thinner binding, and lower profile height.
5. Darker reddish brown rim color on earlier style 3's, changes to more honey wheat color on later examples on into the style 75's.
6. "Pat. Applied For" stamped inside rim vertically close to heel until approx. 1936 or 37.
7. Long nut on bottom coordinator rod in most until approx. 9700's serial number range.
8. 5th string nuts are more finely turned on the lathe with a small lip, and are usually taller in height.
9. Four digit serial numbers, with lot number stamped inside rim on all until approx.9900.
10. Serial number painted in red, and lot number in chalk inside resonator positioned to the right of heel cut, and chalk in the middle of resonator.
11. Cut Mastertone Labels are more commonly seen on original flatheads, some were originally intended to be archtop rims, but many also have uncut labels.
12. Rims are slightly larger in diameter by a few thousandths up until approximately the 9500 serial number range, and the later smaller diameter flanges will not interchange without altering either rim or inside cut on flange.
13. Lettering cut into Mastertone blocks are generally smaller in height than after 1937 banjos.
14. Frets are generally smaller in size closer to mandolin sized fret wire until approx. 1937.
15. Stain color on style 3's neck's and resonators are a little lighter red in color than the later style 3's and 75's.
16. Flathead screws in L-brackets, and truss rod covers.
17. Smaller knurls on thumbscrews.
18. Grover tuners featured on all models.
19. Platings on the earliest examples can be quite rough and can have a blistered appearance. Flanges also tend to pull up easily and crack more easily up until approx. 1935.
20. Most things mentioned are consistently featured on nearly every banjo from this period.

LATE 1930'S TO EARLY 1940'S

1. Less consistency overall, as far as finish color, inlay patterns, and model designations. Starting with style 75 banjos in 1937, there are many variations as to wood type, inlay patterns, finish color, metal plating. Several Toptension models will also not conform 100% to standard catalog variety. This was mainly due to trying to fill factory orders

while being in short supply of materials in the years preceding and during WWII.

2. Two dots at the 12th fret on side binding on most.

3. Thicker binding in both height, and width.

4. Heavier clear coat of nitrocellulose creating different cracking patterns in finish than earlier 30's models.

5. No "Pat. Applied For" stamping in rims after approx. 1937.

6. Changed from 4 digit serial numbers in rim, starting with the number 1 in approx. mid 1935-1936, going to 3 digit numbers only throughout approx.1937. Also there were three distinctly different die cast number stamps used at this time. There is no apparent reason for this, but the rarest form are seen mainly on a few top tensions with numbers still stamped inside the rim.

7. Changed again to no serial numbers in rim, and stamping them into back of peghead approx. 1938.

8. Serial numbers in resonator changed from red paint to all chalk approx. 1937.

9. Most Serial numbers in back of peghead have letter prefixes beginning with D, DA, E, EA, F, FA, and a few others are seen such a G. Number can be 3, or 4 digits with or without lot number, but most have lot numbers. Some very late examples have no sign of a serial number anywhere.

10. Uncut Mastertone labels inside the rim are more common in original flatheads from this period, but some never had a label at all.

11. Lettering cut in Mastertone blocks of this period are generally taller and larger than the early 30's banjos.

12. Frets are of a larger size than the early 30's banjos.

13. Stain color is generally darker on necks and resonators on transitional style 3 and later 75 banjos.

14. Larger knurls on thumbscrews in later banjos, approx. 1938 on, but not always.

15. Lighter reddish honey wheat color rim in style 75 banjos.

16. Kluson tuners with amber buttons replaced the Grover pancakes on most all style 75 banjos, and several other models approx. 1939. Grover's are still found on a few banjos after this change though for whatever reason.

17. Later 5th string nuts are shorter, flatter, and less lathe turned and generally plainer than earlier 1930's examples.

18. Several style75 banjos are noted with E, EA, F, and FA serial number prefixes that came factory original with mahogany resonators, and maple necks with no handstop. Most of these have a fleur delis inlay in the peghead, with a large fat "Gibson" inlay. Also there are several style 75, and toptension models noted with mixed and interchanged inlay patterns, plating's, and wood types .

19. Many of these late 30's, early 40's style 75 banjos also have chrome plated flathead tonerings with the rest of the metal being nickel plated.

20. Several late style 3, early transitional style 75 banjos have rare inlay patterns such as full Flying Eagle inlay, and Flying Eagle with a style 3/75 peghead inlay now known as the "Reno pattern", also the Wreath pattern, Flying Eagle, Hearts and Flowers, Bella Voce, and other odd inlay combinations are known.

21. Plating continued to get better after approx. 1935 and was generally great in the later years. Flanges also tend to remain stronger and flatter.

ONLY ORIGINAL "MASTERTONE" FINGERPICK I'VE BEEN ABLE TO FIND, AND IS AN EXACT MATE TO THE #92 FINGERPICK IN THE PRE WAR GIBSON CATALOGS.

Other Stuff Besides Banjos

THESE 5 WRENCHES ARE THE MOST COMMONLY FOUND TO EXIST WITH 100% ALL ORIGINAL BANJOS, AND WOULD HAVE COME AS STANDARD EQUIPMENT IN THE CASE POCKET WITH ANY NEWLY PURCHASED GIBSON BANJO

GROVER "TWO BAND" STYLE, GOLD PLATED WITH ORIGINAL SOLID PEARL BUTTONS

GROVER "TWO BAND" STYLE, NICKEL PLATED WITH IVOROID BUTTONS

1935

1936

1937

1938 THRU 1941. SAME CATALOG WITH UPDATED PRICES.

1942 THRU WWII.

ORIGINAL GIBSON CATALOGS FROM 1935 TO 1942

GROVER "PANCAKE" STYLE, WITH IVOROID BUTTONS

SMALLER MORE COMMON KLUSON STYLE, WITH AMBER BUTTONS, SEEN ON MANY LATER STYLE 75's

ALL FACTORY ACCESSORIES INCLUDED WITH THE "POSIE ROACH" RB-75 INCLUDING, #521 GREEN FLANNEL "REDLINE" HARDSHELL CASE, ORIGINAL CASE KEY AND FACTORY ENVELOPE, ORIGINAL BRACKET WRENCH, INSTRUCTIONAL PAPER FROM GIBSON ON SET UP AND MAINTENANCE OF YOUR NEW BANJO, AND ALSO A BRAND NEW SET OF GIBSON BANJO STRINGS! DON'T FORGET THAT EXPENSIVE $3.00 FACTORY OPTION, THE GIBSON HEADGUARD!

RARE LARGER "STAIR STEP" KLUSON STYLE, WITH AMBER BUTTON TUNERS, MORE COMMONLY SEEN ON LATER TOPTENSION AND ELECTRIC GIBSON BANJOS

PLECTRUM BANJOS

GIBSON has done more than put a longer neck on a Tenor Banjo — they have designed and built a Plectrum Banjo with special constructional features that distinguish Gibson Plectrum Banjos from all others—that twangy, brilliant harmony of the plectrum is amplified and enriched. All Gibson plectrum banjos have full 27" scale with 22 frets — tuned D B G C.

Plectrum Banjo
Style PB-Granada

MASTERTONE STYLE PB-6

$300.00

CASE: No. 522 Faultless $22.00

Gold plated and engraved metal parts—beautiful burl walnut woods — special plectrum banjo rim construction—27" scale and 22 frets—for detailed description see tenor banjo style TB-6 on page 32, just the same with exception of neck and rim.

UNCLE DAVE MACON
Radio-Records

GIBSON PLECTRUM AND FIVE-STRING BANJO RIM CONSTRUCTION

The special rim construction on Gibson plectrum and 5 string banjos assures players sweeter tone and greater volume.

PAGE FROM THE 1935 GIBSON CATALOG "W."

The First Appearance of the Flathead Tonering in Print and Standard Factory Production

If we look at all printed catalog descriptions regarding Mastertone banjos before the 1930 Gibson catalog which was the first to feature the new one piece flange designed Mastertone banjos, there is absolutely no mention whatsoever of any difference in tone chamber, or rim construction for any model of Mastertone banjo, including the Tenor, Plectrum, or (RB, meaning regular or 5 string) designations. They are all listed as being exactly the same in overall rim construction, with the only difference being the tenor, plectrum, or five string necks. The earliest documentation in print to the public comes in the Blue 1930 Gibson catalog which mentions on the page featuring "Gibson Fivestring Banjos", a "flat type head, single bearing, for fivestring banjos", it also on the same page quickly contradicts itself by saying in the upper part of the ad that.. "The original banjo made modern full 27" scale length with extra fifth string, otherwise constructed like tenor banjos. It then goes on to list the RB-1, 11, 3, 4, and "G" for Granada. The next several Gibson catalogs are pretty much the same as this early one in their descriptions. The Gibson catalog "W" of 1935 is the first Gibson catalog to announce in its descriptions of Mastertone banjos, "special rim construction" on all plectrum, and RB, or 5 string models. It goes so far as to say that "Gibson has done more than put a longer neck on a tenor banjo" speaking of their latest Plectrum banjos with its "special constructional features" as you can see from this 1935 catalog quote. This is undoubtedly the first mention to the public, and is absolutely the first documented proof that Gibson was installing a production line, standard catalog version, factory original, flathead tonering in these particular Plectrum and Fivestring Mastertone banjos from approximately 1934 on. They were still very low on the production list as very few were ordered anyway when compared with standard tenor banjos. Several plectrums and a very few fivestrings were ordered and featured the flathead tonering at this time. At the bottom of this same page it says...**Gibson Plectrum and Fivestring Banjo Rim Construction,** "The special rim construction on Gibson Plectrum and Fivestring banjos assures players sweeter tone and greater volume". The actual Flathead Tonering, or "Tone Chamber" as they called it, was mentioned in many, now very rare letters and documents that were sent to Gibson dealers, and representatives only, but in these pages we are only discussing public announcements, such as brochures, and Gibson catalogs that were available to the public.

Several pre war Gibson banjo authorities, and collectors have stated in print for many years that Gibson only installed factory flathead tonerings in a very few banjos, strictly as a "custom option" in these early years, and also that the Gibson company never mentioned anything at all in print concerning a standard production flathead tonering until 1937, with the advent of the Toptension banjos in catalog "Y" of 1937. I have to disagree and chalk this up to a general lack of information concerning these details in the past, and also because of the many advances that have been made in documenting these details in only the last 10 years. I firmly believe that the installation of standard production flathead tonerings was no custom option at all, and by 1935 was a standard factory procedure on

99.9% of plectrum and 5 string banjos from approx. 1934 on into the war years. If you don't agree with me, see how many original plectrums, or original 5 string Mastertone banjos you can find made after 1935 with an original archtop ring. There are a few, but they are certainly the minority, not the flatheads. As I say, 99% of these banjos are original flatheads. I believe this is because Gibson was trying to capture a market in something other than the waning tenor banjo market, and the plectrum players didn't particularly like the thinner sound of the archtop ring. They preferred the deeper tone of the flathead ring, as it was more responsive to the longer scaled fingerboard of the plectrum, and since the scale of the 5 stringed, RB models were exactly the same scale length, it was certainly logical to use them there as well.

Most people deep into the study of these particular banjos have read over the descriptions and quotes in both the old original Gibson catalogs, and brochures of the 30's and 40's, and also the newer reproductions of these catalogs available today. The problem is that most have never seen the forest for the trees. They didn't deeply study what they were actually reading. It has been right in front of their eyes the whole time. I ask you sincerely.. What else can "special rim construction" truly mean? The **one and only** difference concerning an archtop or flathead banjo's rim construction is the **tonering** itself. The wood rim, resonator, coordinator rods, flange, armrest, brackets and nuts, tensionhoop, and just right down to every nut, bolt, screw and washer, are all exactly the same, in both the archtop and flathead banjos. This is an absolute in every Mastertone banjo from this period with a one piece flange. Therefore I hope that you'll agree with me when I say, that the only thing "special rim construction" can possibly mean, without spelling it out, is the addition of a factory installed, standard production, flathead tonering, **period**, end of story.

The main thing that has caused much confusion with early catalogs is that the Gibson Company didn't believe in spending money foolishly updating photo engravings in their future catalogs for something as simple as a Tonering change, so they didn't change them, Ever!, even though these photos were completely outdated. This has caused quite a bit of confusion over the years by people believing that all the photos in the catalogs were up to date modern examples for a specific period. The Gibson Co. used the same set of photos portraying all there banjos, (excluding the Toptensions), with archtop tonerings from the original 1930 catalogs photo engravings through every catalog produced in the 1930's. On the photo for the 5 string RB- 3, and also the RB- 75 as late as the 1940 "AA" catalog, they actually used a photo of a 2 piece flange, archtop model RB-3! So don't pay a lot of attention to the photos, **read the written descriptions.**

Gibson had actually used the term "Tone Chamber" in print as early as 1936, concerning their Plectrum and Fivestring Mastertone banjos in Gibson's catalog " X". However, the company didn't really tout this new "Tone Chamber" to any degree, in print to the public until 1937, with the new Gibson catalog "Y", featuring the totally new designed, more modern line of Toptension banjos, and also debuting the budget model 75. Starting a new in 1937, the Gibson Company basically phased out all standard pot construction Mastertone models such as the style 3, 4, 6, Granada, Bella Voce, Florentine, and All American and debuted the newly designated "Style 75", which had previously been known as the style 3. I personally believe that someone in the advertising department at the Gibson Company just decided the term "Tone Chamber", was a nice sounding catchy little slogan, and decided to showcase an older idea that had already been in use for several years, aka the Flathead Tonering. "Tone Chamber" surely appeared much nicer in print with the new more stylish Art Deco inspired Gibson Top Tension designed banjos, and it certainly sounded more modern and hip, than "special rim construction".

This 1937 "Y" catalog also featured many newer improved idea's of the day, such as the first of Gibson's new electric guitars, Hawaiian Lap-steels, amplifiers, and also factory pickups to convert your older Acoustic guitars to Electric. It even featured an entirely new line of electric mandolins, and banjos.

So you see this was a happening time in America, and new ad campaigns for all types of commodities were all the rage. The relatively new Art Deco design was in full swing throughout the US, as it was very popular. Many of New York's most famous Skyscrapers were being newly built at this time, and it's easy to see this modern line of new toptension banjos were surely designed with this Deco style in mind. It seems Gibson needed their banjos to appear totally different from the standard older type rim construction model Mastertone banjos of the mid 30's, and this whole 1937 catalog was stepping out for them, so maybe the Company thought the mention of this newer improved "Tone Chamber" would look like a winner to consumers!

Unfortunately for all banjo manufacturers, they had no way of knowing that their days were numbered, for in just a few short years the newer larger bodied archtop guitars would completely takeover the market in most all types of music where the once loved tenor and plectrum banjo had been played. It seems a few older classical banjoists, and some hillbilly's with good steady jobs were responsible for the very few 5 string flathead Mastertone banjos ordered throughout this period.

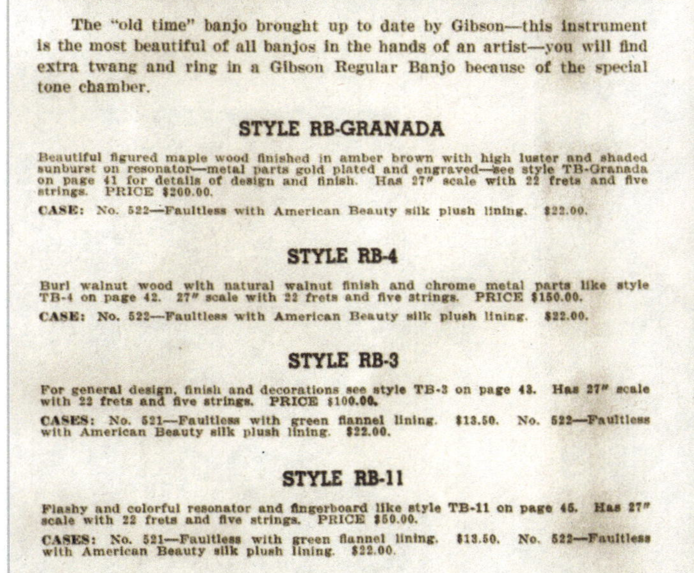

REGULAR OR 5 STRING BANJOS

The "old time" banjo brought up to date by Gibson—this instrument is the most beautiful of all banjos in the hands of an artist—you will find extra twang and ring in a Gibson Regular Banjo because of the special tone chamber.

STYLE RB-GRANADA

Beautiful figured maple wood finished in amber brown with high luster and shaded sunburst on resonator—metal parts gold plated and engraved—see style TB-Granada on page 41 for details of design and finish. Has 27" scale with 22 frets and five strings. PRICE $200.00.

CASE: No. 522—Faultless with American Beauty silk plush lining. $22.00.

STYLE RB-4

Burl walnut wood with natural walnut finish and chrome metal parts like style TB-4 on page 42. 27" scale with 22 frets and five strings. PRICE $150.00.

CASE: No. 522—Faultless with American Beauty silk plush lining. $22.00.

STYLE RB-3

For general design, finish and decorations see style TB-3 on page 43. Has 27" scale with 22 frets and five strings. PRICE $100.00.

CASES: No. 521—Faultless with green flannel lining. $13.50. No. 522—Faultless with American Beauty silk plush lining. $22.00.

STYLE RB-11

Flashy and colorful resonator and fingerboard like style TB-11 on page 45. Has 27" scale with 22 frets and five strings. PRICE $50.00.

CASES: No. 521—Faultless with green flannel lining. $13.50. No. 522—Faultless with American Beauty silk plush lining. $22.00.

STYLE RB-1

See style TB-1 on page 47 for design, finish and decorations. Has 27" scale with 22 frets and five strings. PRICE $37.50.

CASES: No. 521—Faultless with green flannel lining. $13.50. No. 522—Faultless with American Beauty silk plush lining. $22.00.

STYLE RB-00

So that anyone can own a genuine Gibson regular banjo, we have created this fine model for only $27.50. Similar to style TB-00 on page 48 except has 27" scale with 22 frets and five strings. PRICE $27.50.

CASE: No. 121—Challenge, side opening—green flannel lining. $5.00.

[51]

STYLE RB-3
$100.00

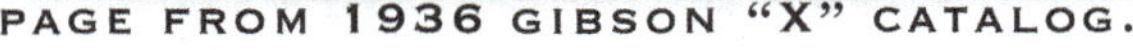

PAGE FROM 1936 GIBSON "X" CATALOG.

They would remain relatively dormant for the next 10 years or more until Mr. Earl Scruggs began using them exclusively, creating almost singlehandedly, a powerful demand for them all over the country again.

If you're considering buying, selling or trading any Pre-War Gibson Banjo, or related parts, please call or email Jim Mills first. I can travel anywhere, and I pay good prices promptly. I buy, sell, trade, and collect.
Phone- 919-608-0355
Email- jimmillsbanjo@msn.com
"I constantly strive to keep the largest selection of 1930s 1 piece flange, pre-war Gibson conversion banjos for sale at all times. I have over 20 years experience trading, and collecting these fine instruments, and I provide full authentication, and a personal set-up on all banjos I sell."
Satisfaction Guaranteed
Sincerely, Jim Mills
Original Flathead Fivestring RB-75 with rare, factory original full flying eagle inlay pattern Sn. 445-4 ca. 1937
Original Flathead Fivestring RB-75 Sn. EA-5691 ca. 1939
One of a kind Factory Original Gold plated Flathead Fivestring RB-75 Sn. F-453-2 ca. 1940
"Snuffy Jenkins" Original Flathead Fivestring RB-4 Sn. 9639-1 ca. 1934
ca. 1936 One of a kind original fivestring RB-1 with factory original RB-3 fingerboard Sn. 213-3
GIBSON